NORTH | SOUTH | EAST | WEST

American Indians and the Natural World

Marsha C. Bol

TOM BARR, PRINCIPAL PHOTOGRAPHER

CARNEGIE MUSEUM OF NATURAL HISTORY

AND ROBERTS RINEHART PUBLISHERS

PITTSBURGH AND BOULDER

Copyright ©1998 Carnegie Institute

International Standard Book Number

1-57098-094-2 (cb)

1-57098-197-3 (pb)

Library of Congress Cataloging-in-Publication Data

Bol, Marsha.

 North, South, East, West : Native Americans and
 the natural world / Marsha C. Bol.

  p. cm.

 Includes bibliographical references and index.
 ISBN 1-57098-094-2. — ISBN 1-57098-197-3 (pbk).
 1. Indians of North America–Material culture–Catalogs.
 2. Indians of North America–Social life and
 customs–Catalogs. 3. Indians of North
 America–Antiquities–Catalogs. 4. Carnegie Museum of
 Natural History. Alcoa Foundation Hall of American
 Indians–Catalogs. I. Title
 E98.M34B65 1998
 973' .0497–dc21   98–5094
                 CIP

PUBLISHED BY

ROBERTS RINEHART PUBLISHERS

6309 MONARCH PARK PLACE

NIWOT, COLORADO 80503

Distributed to the trade by
Publishers Group West

PUBLISHED IN IRELAND
AND THE UK BY

ROBERTS RINEHART PUBLISHERS

TRINITY HOUSE, CHARLESTON ROAD

DUBLIN 6, IRELAND

Published in cooperation with
Carnegie Museum of Natural History

COPYRIGHT PAGE ILLUSTRATION:
An Iroquois baby wrapped in a floral beaded baby carrier,
1872. (Photographer unknown. Buffalo and Erie County
Historical Society)

CONTENTS PAGE ILLUSTRATION:
A Hopi woman shells kernels of dried corn, ca. 1905-1912.
(Photo by Kate Cory. Museum of Northern Arizona Photo
Archives, MS208/75.881)

SECTION DIVIDER ILLUSTRATIONS:
Tom Barr, Iroquois and Urban; Melinda McNaugher, Tlingit
and Lakota; Owen Seumptewa, Hopi.

DESIGN: CAROL HARALSON

Foreword

THE ALCOA FOUNDATION HALL of American Indians opened to the public in June 1998. The opening of any major exhibition is a monumental event in the life of a city. The excitement over this particular hall has been magnetic, rippling out from Carnegie Museum of Natural History staff, Board members, donors, and American Indian consultants to the surrounding community and beyond.

The museum's dream for a new hall depicting the life of American Indians up to the present day arose from a self-study grant awarded in 1984 by the National Endowment for the Humanities (NEH). The resultant study brought to the fore the need to make available to the public the museum's exciting Ancient Egyptian and American Indian artifacts. After the Walton Hall of Ancient Egypt opened in 1990, visions for the new Hall of American Indians evolved under the leadership of Director James E. King. Implementation grants from Alcoa Foundation (1989) and NEH (1994) spurred on plans for the hall. Since these initial grants, numerous foundations and individuals have generously contributed, making the hall a reality.

The museum was fortunate to bring Marsha C. Bol on board in 1990 to curate the hall. Dr. Bol has brought her scholarly background and extensive museum experience to the project. She has also brought great enthusiasm.

"Carnegie's amazing Native American collection, tucked away in the Section of Anthropology, is one of the great remaining secrets, and I am excited that the public is now able to view one thousand of our most-important artifacts."

In developing the hall, we relied on the expert guidance of our museum staff. Key players included Dr. James B. Richardson III, Curator, Section of Anthropology; Joan S. Gardner, Anthopology Conservator; James R. Senior, Chairman, Division of Exhibit Design and Production; and Dianne Folsom, Education Coordinator for the hall. Sixteen members from the Division of Exhibits worked full-time for the final ten months of production on the hall. Many other staff members, too numerous to mention, contributed to the creation of the hall. For all of us the development of the hall has been a tremendously uplifting experience.

The Alcoa Foundation Hall of American Indians could never have been completed without our fourteen knowledgeable and creative Native American consultants and other scholars. They have guided us all along the way, helped us to understand their cultures more fully, and brought strong Native voices and perspectives throughout the hall. We from the museum have been enriched by the professional partnerships and friendships that have developed with these consultants. Our heartfelt thanks go to Hartman Lomaiwaima, Hopi section;

Bea Medicine and Nellie Star Boy Menard, Lakota section; Joe Medicine Crow, Crow section; Nora Dauenhauer, Tlingit section; DuWayne Bowen and Ron LaFrance, Iroquois section; Charles Burrell, Michele Leonard, Lisa Mitten, Tomi Simms, and Pamela Soeder, urban section; Tsianina Lomawaima, education section; and Rayna Green, entire project.

The consultants were also a part of the team that developed *North, South, East, West: American Indians and the Natural World,* by Marsha C. Bol. This catalogue's full-color images of our most important artifacts are accompanied with statements by American Indians interwoven together by Dr. Bol's adept hand. As consultant Hartman Lomawaima expressed so succinctly, *"North, South, East, West* presents more than a series of glimpses of American Indian lives and material culture. It brings a level of emotion that will surely grab the reader."

The Alcoa Foundation Hall of American Indians and this accompanying catalogue offer a special opportunity to Pittsburgh and beyond, an opportunity not only to view many wonderful artifacts but to meet the people who made and used them.

JAY APT, DIRECTOR
Carnegie Museum of Natural History

Lakota youths enjoy a leisurely Sunday afternoon, 1970s. (Photo by Don Doll)

NATIVE VISIONS OF THE NATURAL WORLD

AMERICAN INDIANS have their own ways of relating to the natural world. This is not a new concept. In fact, it has been coined into a series of much-used cliches in twentieth-century American society, all proclaiming that Indian people are "close to nature" or "at one with nature." Yet what do most of us non-Natives really know about the foundations of this concept beyond our automatic association of Indian people with the world of nature? For example, are we familiar with the connection that Lakota people have with the constellations, that the stars create a connected response from life on the planet to life in the heavens?

In Lakota we have an expression that goes "As it is above, so it is below." It means that when the stars and constellations are moving in their place, we the two-leggeds respond . . . and so the pattern that we create on the ground as we migrate is the same as the pattern in the sky.

ROBERT OWENS, LAKOTA, 1997 [1]

Plains Indians visit Carnegie Museum, May 4, 1910. Performers in the 101 Ranch Wild West Show take a break from their Pittsburgh performance to see the sights at the museum.
(Carnegie Museum of Natural History, 14351-36)

This is, indeed, a different way of thinking about the night sky than that of the majority of Americans.

In 1990, Rayna Green, director of the American Indian Program at the National Museum of American History and consultant for our new Hall of American Indians, challenged our exhibit team to take as the hall's theme the relationship of American Indians with the natural world. This topic is thoroughly appropriate to our mission as a natural history museum. Native people themselves point with pride to their on-going heritage of connections with the natural universe and have been extremely supportive of our approach.

We set out to question the foundations of this theme, to examine three aspects of it. First, what practical knowledge do Native peoples employ in collaborating with

Opposite: Treva Burton of the Hopi village of Oraibi collects rabbit brush (*Chrysothamnus naseosus*), 1991. It will be used as the dyed weft in wicker baskets made by women of Third Mesa.
(Photo by Helga Teiwes. Arizona State Museum, #85864)

Oglala Sioux Ceremony, 1907. A sacred buffalo skull, resting on a bed of sage, occupies the place of honor. (Photo by Edward S. Curtis. National Anthropological Archives, Smithsonian Institution, 55-940)

their environments? We look at the collection and use of plants; techniques used in fishing, hunting, and agriculture; methods of processing foods and arts; observing the stars; and controlling and manipulating the environment. Next, what basic philosophies and understandings do Indian people share concerning the relationships of all inhabitants of the universe to one another and how they all should be treated? For example, we examine the reciprocal and respectful relationship between the hunter and the hunted, including game animals, fish, plants, rain water, minerals, and clay. This theme is fundamental to any interaction of Native peoples with their environment, and no consideration of the links between Indian people and nature can exclude this perspective. And finally, how has the natural universe been altered by ecological and social changes initiated through human interactions and competition?

Within the pages of this book are five different visions of living in and with the natural world—those of the Hopi, Lakota, Tlingit, Iroquois, and urban Indians. Of course, there are many others, as diverse as the American Indian nations themselves. We selected the visions of these five different cultural groups because of the strengths of our collections and our decision to represent a range of diverse regional environments. Respected members of each of these five communities worked with us and guided our efforts to unfold the groups' strategies for relating with their natural surroundings. Each of these groups has a long and complex history that cannot be served adequately in a few pages, so our historical time frame emphasizes the nineteenth and

A Lakota woman used porcupine quills like the ones below to decorate this moccasin ca. 1890s. (See page 114).

twentieth centuries, particularly the last one hundred years. The connections of Native peoples with their natural universe not only were operable in the precontact past, but have continued to be important and viable into the late twentieth century. Although the material aspects may have altered, the philosophical relationships remain meaningful.

To the Tlingit people, home is the narrow coastal beaches of southeast Alaska, where their lives revolve around the harvest from the sea. For the Hopi people of the high mesas of Arizona, corn is life. Agriculture is not easy, yet the Hopi farm successfully in their arid and demanding homeland. In the Dakotas, the Lakota people, who converged on horseback onto the central Plains to hunt game animals, visualize a cosmic family of humans, bison, elk, and other relatives. To the Iroquois nations, the Three Sisters—corn, beans, and squash—are the major sustainers of life, one and the same with the women, the lineage, and the continuity of society. Today, more than 60 percent of the total American Indian population reside in urban areas, making cities and suburbs an environment of considerable importance in Native American life.

Although all of these peoples have chosen different pathways and strategies for making a life in their various environments, one concept is voiced by all. It is expressed by the Lakota people at the end of every ceremony with the phrase *all my relatives.*

Abalone shells are inlaid in Northwest Coast wooden masks, frontlets, and other family treasures.

Adam Spring with his crop of pumpkins and drying braids of corn at Tonawanda Reservation. (Photographer and date unknown. Rochester Museum and Science Center, Rochester, New York, 1958)

Famed Haida chief Sonihat and his family pose with their heirlooms in their house at Kasaan, Alaska, pre-1912. (Photographer unknown. James B. Richardson III)

Iroquois Deer Clan Mother Audrey Shenandoah with daughters Midwife Jessica Jeanne Shenandoah, seated, and Rochell Brown, 1991. (Photo by Toba Pato Tucker)

A Hopi wedding, 1977. Female family and friends of the bride try on her robe and reed suitcase after her return from the groom's home in the village of Kykotsmovi. (Photo by Owen Seumptewa)

Cotton bolls. The traditional Hopi wedding robe is woven of native-grown cotton. Cotton was introduced from Central America via Mexico in ancient times.

Everything is related. As Indian people have developed and evolved throughout the ages, we have done so alongside all of these other creatures—buffalo, prairie dogs, eagles—all these different things that we learned from. We recognized the importance of all these other things and that the people were only part of this grand scheme, not any better, not any worse, but just a major part of it. So one of the terms that we used to describe that is translated as "all my relatives." And that's what the spiritual essence of Indian people is, that connection to the rest of the world.

FRED DuBRAY, LAKOTA, 1994[2]

In the longhouse, an Iroquois elder recites the Thanksgiving Address. The address expresses the family or kinship relationship between the people and the other elements in the universe, including the Three Sisters, the trees and other plants, the animals, the birds, the water, the stars, and the wind.

Those who take care of them [the Three Sisters] every day asked that they be sisters. And at that time there arose a relationship between them: we shall say "the Sisters, our sustenance."

CORBETT SUNDOWN, TONAWANDA SENECA, 1959[3]

As Santa Clara Pueblo women prepare to make their pots, they say a prayer to Clay-Old-Lady. *Give me good thoughts as I am making this pot. We are in partnership. I can't make it without your help,* petitions Tessie Naranjo, Santa Clara Pueblo, 1996. All things have life. Clay also has life, and necessarily we develop a relationship with clay.[4]

Everywhere across Native North America, traditional Indian people rise in the morning saying a prayer that recognizes their connectedness with the universe, and this relationship begins anew.

TO PLAN A LONG-TERM EXHIBITION and a catalogue encompassing American Indian cultures north of Mexico is an ambitious undertaking. Such an enterprise involves enough people to populate a village. At the forefront stand the tradition-bearers and scholars from all over the country who have shared their cultural and historical knowledge as well as their personal experiences. I would like to give special thanks to each and every one of the following consultants for their guidance, generosity, patience, and honesty: DuWayne Bowen, Jerry Brody, David Brumble, Charles Burrell, Joe Medicine Crow, Nora Marks Dauenhauer, Richard Dauenhauer, Rayna Green, Bill Holm, Fran King, Ron LaFrance, Michele Leonard, Rosalie Little Thunder, Hartman Lomawaima, Tsianina Lomawaima, Beatrice Medicine, Nellie Star Boy Menard, Lisa Mitten, Tomi Simms, Pam Soeder, Richard White, Andrew Whiteford, and Ray Williamson. We were greatly saddened at the sudden death of Ron LaFrance in 1996. Ron contributed immeasurably to the Iroquois section of the exhibit.

Many other Indian people also contributed their talents, energy, and ideas. Special thanks go to Anne Arnold, Florentine Blue Thunder, Lisa Boots, Fred Deer, Amy Good Bear, Ernestine Hanlon, Tom Haukaas, LaVonne Honyouti, Loretta Secakuku Jenkins, Micah Jenkins, Ramson Lomatewama, Bill Menard, Monica Nuvamsa, Kenneth Poocha, Owen Seumptewa, Skye Seumptewa, Russell Simms, Kelly Star Chief, Blythe Suetopka, Cathy Young, and Victor Young.

As part of this project, we initiated an internship for Native students with an interest in museum studies. Each of our interns—Kawenniiosta "Yosta" Boots, Pamela Creasy, Ramona Medicine Crow, and Pollyanna Nordstrand—made a significant contribution to the exhibition.

Many volunteers generously donated their time. I am especially grateful to Joan Becker, Martha Clift, Walter Clift, Jean Henry, Hazel Johnson, and Heather Oblak, who searched through unread letters and documents in the museum's archives, researched tough questions, transcribed oral interview tapes, and sewed clothing for the exhibition mannequins.

As the largest exhibit to be created in the museum's hundred-year history, this project dominated the affairs of the Section of Anthropology for eight years. I would like to thank the staff members who not only participated in its planning but also lived with the disruption. Section chairman James B. Richardson III, who initially ignited the project,

Button from a boy's uniform worn at the Carlisle Indian School. (See page 138.)

Two young Tlingit girls stand in front of drying salmon at their family's summer fish camp, Yukon River, Alaska, ca. 1898-1920. (Photo by W. H. Case and H. H. Draper. Alaska State Library, 39-177)

Iroquois children in traditional clothing. (Photographer and date unknown. Iroquois Indian Museum, IIM 94.32A.36A)

Andrew Soeder at Council of Three Rivers American Indian Powwow, 1992. (Photo by Marsha C. Bol)

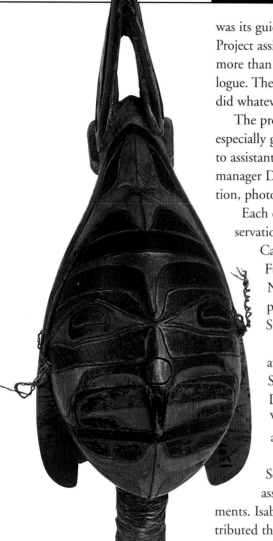

Tlingit raven rattle.
(See pages 16-17.)

was its guiding light and a good-humored partner throughout its development. Project assistants Melissa Elsberry, Sylvia Keller, and Beth Worstell devoted much more than their workday hours to the successful completion of this exhibit and catalogue. They worried, they cared, they missed dinner and lost sleep. In essence, they did whatever was necessary, or even possible, to bring the project to reality.

The process of documenting the collections took several years to complete. I am especially grateful to curatorial assistants Barbara Aimino and Anne Roskell, as well as to assistant curator Marilee Schmit, for taking on this monumental task. Collections manager Deborah Harding lent a helping hand at every stage, including documentation, photographing, and handling of the artifacts before the exhibit cases were sealed.

Each of the some 1,000 artifacts selected for display in the exhibit required conservation analysis and treatment. Chief conservator Joan Gardner, assisted by Scott Carroll, Virginia Greene, and Rhonda Wozniak and consultants Tamsen Fuller and Lisa Mibach, conserved this vast and diverse group of objects. Neither snow nor sleet, not evenings nor weekends slowed these dedicated professionals. Thanks also go to interns Caird Harbeck and Margaret Stremple-Breuker.

The project benefited immeasurably from the diverse scientific expertise available in Carnegie Museum of Natural History. Kenneth Parkes in the Section of Birds, Fred Utech and Sue Thompson in the Section of Botany, Duane Schlitter and Sue McLaren in the Section of Mammals, and Marc Wilson in the Section of Minerals identified materials in the artifacts and advised on content questions.

The exhibit's design and construction were in the able hands of James Senior, chairman of the Division of Exhibit Design and Production, and assistant chairman Patrick Martin, who fabricated the dioramas and environments. Isabelle Nardelli was responsible for overall design while many others contributed their special talents. Neil Rossi detailed exhibit construction. Lorraine Czolba, Kemon Lardas, Nancy Perkins, and Gail Richards produced graphics. Mark Barill, Heidi Carroll, Donald Cromer, Frank Davis, Robert Johnson, Ron Lutz II, Russell North, and Daniel Pickering added creative fabrication skills. Melinda McNaugher produced photographic images, while John Bauer and William May installed electrical components. Thanks also to volunteer Henry Yocco and students Lauren Eckie, Patrick Monahan, and April Wilson.

Independent filmmaker Pat Ferrero produced nine videos and ten audio segments for the exhibit. It was a pleasure to watch her bring folks' stories and experiences into view and then weave them seamlessly together. I am grateful to those people who shared their stories on camera and tape.

Dianne Folsom was invaluable in developing the educational programs and collaborating on exhibit content. We were most fortunate to have her dedicated contributions as education coordinator to this project. Judith Bobenage, chair of the Division of Education, and her staff developed numerous special programs. Thanks to Diane Grzybek, Patrick McShea, Douglas Patinka, and Pamela St. John. Outside consultant Jeff Hayward conducted audience research that shaped the exhibit outcomes.

Publications editor Louise Craft was the guiding hand behind this book, doing everything from securing funding to completing the editing and production after she retired. Through her knowledge of publishing and her watchful eye, she has served as midwife throughout the arduous process of birthing this catalogue. Tom Barr shot the artifact photographs for the catalogue, ever considerate of the integrity of the objects. Carol Haralson brought the book to life with her comprehending, joyful design. Carol spent hundreds of hours refining every detail of the complex design so the book's color, form, and imagery faithfully convey its contents. Our thanks to Rick Rinehart and Betsy Armstrong of Roberts Rinehart Publishers for their warm-spirited collaboration.

I am especially grateful to former director James E. King for his trust and confidence in our capabilities and to our new director Jay Apt for continuing to support this project. Thanks also to Carolyn Sekerka, Judy Kane, and Gretchen Sulc, who monitored the bottom line.

The Alcoa Foundation provided the lead funding for the exhibition. Special thanks are due to Earl Gadbery, former Alcoa Foundation president; F. Worth Hobbs, president; and Kathleen W. Buechel, vice president, for their encouragement and continued interest throughout the project. The National Endowment for the Humanities contributed substantial funding. I am grateful to program officer Suzi Jones for shepherding us through its process. Other funding was furnished by the Clapp Charitable Trust, the Hopwood Charitable Trust, Torrence M. Hunt, the Massey Charitable Trust, the Mudge Foundation, the Pennsylvania Historic and Museums Commission, the Scaife Family Foundation, and an anonymous contributor. A second anonymous donor funded this publication.

I would especially like to thank my husband, Michael S. Katz, who lived without me for the first several years of our marriage while I worked on this project.

Lightning dance wand. Hopi, collected 1904. Unidentified wood, commercial, and mineral paints, cotton (*Gossypium hirsutum*), immature Golden Eagle feather (*Aquila chrysaetos*), cardboard, tanned hide, steel, commercial cotton; L 38.9 in. (99.0 L x 14.0 W x 2 H cm); Z-9-337

NORTH | SOUTH | EAST | WEST

The Tlingit of the Northwest Coast

NATURE IS LIKE PEOPLE
NATURE IS ALIVE
MOUNTAINS ARE LIKE PEOPLE
TREES ARE LIKE PEOPLE
FISH ARE LIKE PEOPLE
IF MY MOTHER WERE TO MEET A BROWN
BEAR IN THE WOODS,
SHE WOULD SAY:
"MY FATHER'S PEOPLE,
DON'T HARM ME,
MY FATHER'S PEOPLE,
PEACE, PEACE, PEACE"

WALTER SOBOLEFF,
TLINGIT, 1995[1]

WE HAVE A PARTNERSHIP
WITH NATURE

A fisherman never announces that he will go fishing. He just goes out. When he gets to the fishing ground, he baits his hook and starts sinking his line to the bottom . . . spitting on his line as it runs out, telling the halibut, "Here comes your partner to fight with. Won't you jump on him?"

NORA MARKS DAUENHAUER, TLINGIT, 1996[2]

To the coastal Tlingit people, home is the narrow mainland coast, islands, bays, and fjords of southeast Alaska. The people reside on narrow, rocky beaches wedged between the tidewater and dense forests rising into lofty mountains, an area of human occupation for the last 10,000 years. Heavy rainfall creates a luxurious rainforest environment and a temperate climate.

Tlingit villages have always faced the sea. The peoples' lives revolve around the harvest from the sea outside the front door and from the forests and rivers outside the back door. The waters of southeast Alaska provide one of the richest maritime environments in the world. As the Tlingit people make their seasonal rounds, they catch fish and sea mammals and collect shellfish and sea plants.

PARTNERS with Nature

GUESTS ARRIVE IN THEIR CANOE FOR A FUNERAL AT CHIEF SHAKES' DOGFISH HOUSE, WRANGELL, ALASKA, 1886.

(Photo by William H. Partridge. Angelus Collection, University of Oregon Library, AL5 1230)

It was Raven who showed us how to get our food. Raven knew what was good for us and taught the Tlingit how to live, says Austin Hammond, Tlingit.[3]

He open each door. He open the doors for smelts and the smelts comes out from that tank. After that herrings, and oolichons [eulachons], and out of the other sides, king salmon first, and humpies and coho, and later on the one they call the fall fish, dog salmon, and last come the ones that stop, the halibut and flounders and cod, and he pushed them out.

See, just the way [Raven] opened the doors, is just the way they come every year. No mistake on it. And Raven is satisfied, he released all that fish to go around this world.

BILLY WILSON, SR., TLINGIT, 1974[4]

The Pacific salmon is preferred above all other fish. Every year five different species of salmon follow one another in succession, journeying from the sea to swim upriver. From May through September, Tlingit fishermen use spears, hooks, nets, and dams called weirs to catch the salmon.

When the [salmon] run reaches its destina-
tion, it's like a
red blanket,
solid,
with sockeyes. . . .
That whole river is a red blanket,
solid,
mature,
mature sockeyes, eiiih!!!
Boiled fish.

HORACE MARKS, TLINGIT, 1984[5]

Everyone knows that you can eat
just about every part of the salmon
so I don't have to tell you
that you start from the head
because it's everyone's favorite.
You take it apart,
bone by bone. . . .

When done, toss the bones to the ravens
and seagulls, and mosquitoes,
but don't throw them in the salmon stream
because the salmon have spirits
and don't like to see the remains
of their kin thrown in by us
among them in the stream.

NORA MARKS DAUENHAUER, TLINGIT, 1988[6]

Halibut fishing requires the greatest ritual attention because it is the most dangerous fishing activity. The halibut grows to be the largest and most powerful fish in the region.

In the past, fishermen used a specially carved hook, weighted by a rock and suspended downward, so the halibut would see its decoration and be influenced by it. Today Tlingit fishermen still believe that success in fishing depends on the willingness of the fish to make itself available to humans. In selecting the image to carve on the hook, fishermen often chose a powerful creature, perhaps itself a good fisher. Its spirit would entice the fish to the bait.

Practicing respectful observances when fishing for any species, preparing the catch, and eating it continues today as a core Tlingit value. *Your food comes from the land and sea. To abuse either may diminish its generosity,* admonishes Tlingit elder Walter Soboleff.[7]

SCOOPING EULACHON. Tlingit fishermen scoop up hundreds of eulachon with special dip nets during the fish's annual migration from the sea to freshwater rivers to spawn, or lay their eggs.

(Photo by Louis Shotridge, date unknown. University Museum, University of Pennsylvania. 14766)

A TLINGIT FISHERMAN USES A GAFF HOOK TO CATCH A SALMON AT FRESHWATER BAY, ALASKA, 1901.

(Photo by Vincent Soboleff. Alaska State Library, 1-52)

HALIBUT HOOK
Tlingit, pre-1898

The Pacific halibut looks like a fish swimming on its side along the bottom of the sea, except both eyes are on the upper side. It belongs to the flounder family and is by far the largest of all flatfish. Although a halibut can weigh up to 600 pounds, the specially engineered Tlingit hook was designed to catch a fish no larger than a man could haul into his canoe.

The fisherman gave his halibut hook a personal name and carved a figure on it. Then addressing the hook, he said something like, *Go down to halibut land and fight!* [8] The carved image on the hook endowed it with power to lure the fish.

On this hook the wood carver created a land otter, an animal that swims like a fish, has webbed feet like a duck, and, according to Tlingit mythology, was once a human being. As a supernatural being, the land otter steals the spirits of humans who have drowned and entices the living, especially in times of physical weakness.

Yellow cedar *(Chamaecyparis nootkatensis)* or Sitka spruce *(Picea sitchensis),* red alder *(Alnus rubra)* or Pacific yew *(Taxus brevifolia),* Sitka spruce root *(Picea sitchensis),* unidentified bone, cotton cord; L 10.9 in. (27.8 L x 11.5 W x 4.8 H cm); 638-13

FISH CLUB
Kwakwaka'wakw (Kwakiutl), northern Vancouver Island, collected 1904

The fisherman talks first to the hook and then to the halibut after he catches the fish. Before he can lift it on board, he quickly strikes the fish on the head with the heavy club to subdue it. *At the same time he apologizes to the halibut, saying it is not him that strikes, but his hunger.*[9]

The stylized carving on this club may represent a predator. This images adds power to the club.

Pacific yew? *(Taxus brevifolia);* L 22.9 in. (58.2 L x 9.0 D cm); 3178-46

SEAL FEAST BOWL

Tlingit, collected 1904

This feast bowl is carved in the shape of a seal, complete with its head, flippers, and body curve. It was used on special occasions to serve eulachon or seal oil. Oil rendered from the eulachon, a small slender fish, is a prized condiment that is mixed with fish, berries, and other foods. It is also a nutritious dietary supplement, notable for its high vitamin A content.

Red alder *(Alnus rubra)*, abalone shell *(Haliotis* sp); L 12.5 in. (32.0 L x 18.0 W x 12.2 H cm); 3178-63

HEADDRESS

Haida?, collected 1904

This carving of an orca, or killer whale, was worn on the head by a dancer, who could roll its eyes or move its lower jaw during a theatrical performance. No Northwest Coast tribe actively hunted killer whales, the largest members of the dolphin family.

In general, Tlingit people did not hunt whales. Only the southern peoples of the west coast of Vancouver Island and the Washington Olympic Peninsula hunted these animals in large ocean-going canoes.

Cedar?, raw and tanned hide, sea lion whiskers *(Eumetopias jubatus)*, abalone shell *(Haliotis* sp.*)*, iron, mineral paints; L 20.1 in. (51.0 L x 18.1 W x 16.3 H cm); 3178-38

Attracting Game

MOOSE CALL (LEFT)
Cree, Canada, collected ca. 1992

MOOSE CALL (RIGHT)
Northeastern United States, collected pre-1942

Left: Birch bark *(Betula sp.),* unidentified wood; L 22.2 in. (55.6 L x 19 D cm); 35383-1. Right: Birch bark *(Betula papyrifera);* L 15.3 in. (39 L x 7 D cm); 12934-12, gift of Judge James R. McFarlane

CANADA, NEVADA, NORTHEASTERN UNITED STATES

For many Native American cultures, hunting and fishing require not only prowess on the hunter's part, but the animal's willingness to give itself to the man. Native peoples have observed that animals possess abilities that humans do not share. With their superior physical abilities to run, climb, fly, or swim, and their keen senses of sight, smell, and hearing, animals can elude humans if they choose.

Many Native people believe that humans can enter into relationships with animals. They call upon the animal spirits through dreams and prayers for their cooperation in the hunt. The people treat the physical remains of each animal with ceremonial care, so its spirit will assure its kin that it was respectfully treated. In an endeavor to call upon the various animals' capabilities, many hunters decorate tools and weapons with images representing the creatures' power.

DECOY
Ute, Nevada, ca. 1980

Tule reed *(Scirpus* sp.); L 11 in. (28 L x 12.5 W x 21 H cm); 31588, gift of Dr. Craig C. Black

DREAM OF PLENTY
Mable Nigiyok, Holman Island, Northwest Territories, Canada, Inuit, 1992

Paper, ink; W 25.6 in. (53.4 L x 65.4 W cm); 35412-8

The people who call us tree huggers, they're right.

TREES

A GROUP OF TLINGIT WOMEN WEAVE SPRUCE-ROOT BASKETS IN SITKA, ALASKA, 1897.

(Photo by Winter and Pond. Alaska State Library, 87-106)

WE TALK TO THE TREES

We go out to the old growth in the forest with the canopy where the bears sleep and the deer sleep to collect the spruce roots. It feels like you get one real big hug from the trees. The people who call us tree huggers, they're right.

We talk to the trees and we say, "Thank you." It feels good. That's why I feel so threatened with all this logging.

ERNESTINE HANLON, TLINGIT BASKETMAKER, 1995[10]

Dense evergreen forests rise up immediately behind the narrow strips of beach in southeast Alaska. The enormous conifers (cone-bearing trees) are awesome in comparison with humans.
Once the raw materials from the forest provided the basis for nearly everything that the Tlingit used. Before felling a tree, collecting its roots, or removing its bark, the supplicant addressed the tree, saying, *I am here to seek your help.*[11]

TRINKET BASKET (LEFT TO RIGHT)
Tlingit, pre-1923

BASKET
Ernestine Hanlon, Tlingit, Leineid (Raven-Dog Salmon) Clan, Hoonah, Alaska, 1995

BASKET
Tlingit, collected 1904

BERRY BASKET
Tlingit, collected 1904

Our family believed that a girl should begin her life as a weaver at a very young age, ideally at infancy. The girl's fingernails were trimmed and saved to be woven into baskets by her paternal aunts. It's done at dawn, while the Aunty might chant, "Let it be! Let it be!"

As soon as she's able, both maternal and paternal aunts would begin teaching her to weave. The training included gathering [spruce] roots, timothy grass, maiden-hair fern, and dyes; and preparing the materials by splitting roots and dyeing the grasses. When the basket was completed, it was prepared for sale.

NORA MARKS DAUENHAUER, 1981[12]

Tlingit women achieved fame for their finely twined spruce root baskets decorated with dyed grass applied in a technique termed "false embroidery." Wealthy basket collectors sought to augment their collections with Tlingit examples such as the one on the left owned by H. J. Heinz.

There's a few women who still make baskets, but they just don't do it much. It's hard work. It's easier to go to Fred Meyer [supermarket] to just buy plastic bags. . . . The majority of the work is harvesting the roots and the grass, splitting the spruce roots and grass, and dyeing. Weaving the basket is one-fourth of the process. . . .

I also find it more difficult to gather my spruce roots. Hoonah . . . faces mismanaged logging by the U.S. Forest Service as a result of fifteen years of clear-cut areas and a plan to cut the rest of this island.

ERNESTINE HANLON,
TLINGIT, 1995 [13]

(Left to right) Trinket basket: Sitka spruce root *(Picea sitchensis)*, unidentified grass, pebbles?, dye; D 6.8 in. (14.5 H x 17.2 D cm); 8946-11a & b, gift of H. J. Heinz

Basket: Sitka spruce root *(Picea sitchensis)*, unidentified grass, natural dyes; H 6.1 in. (15.5 H x 14.0 D cm); 35989-1

Basket: Sitka spruce root *(Picea sitchensis)*, unidentified grass; D 11.1 in. (27.3 H x 28.2 D cm); 3167-57

Berry basket: Sitka spruce root *(Picea sitchensis)*, unidentified grass, commercial cotton, dye; H 6.9 in. (17.4 H x 13.8 D cm); 3167-16

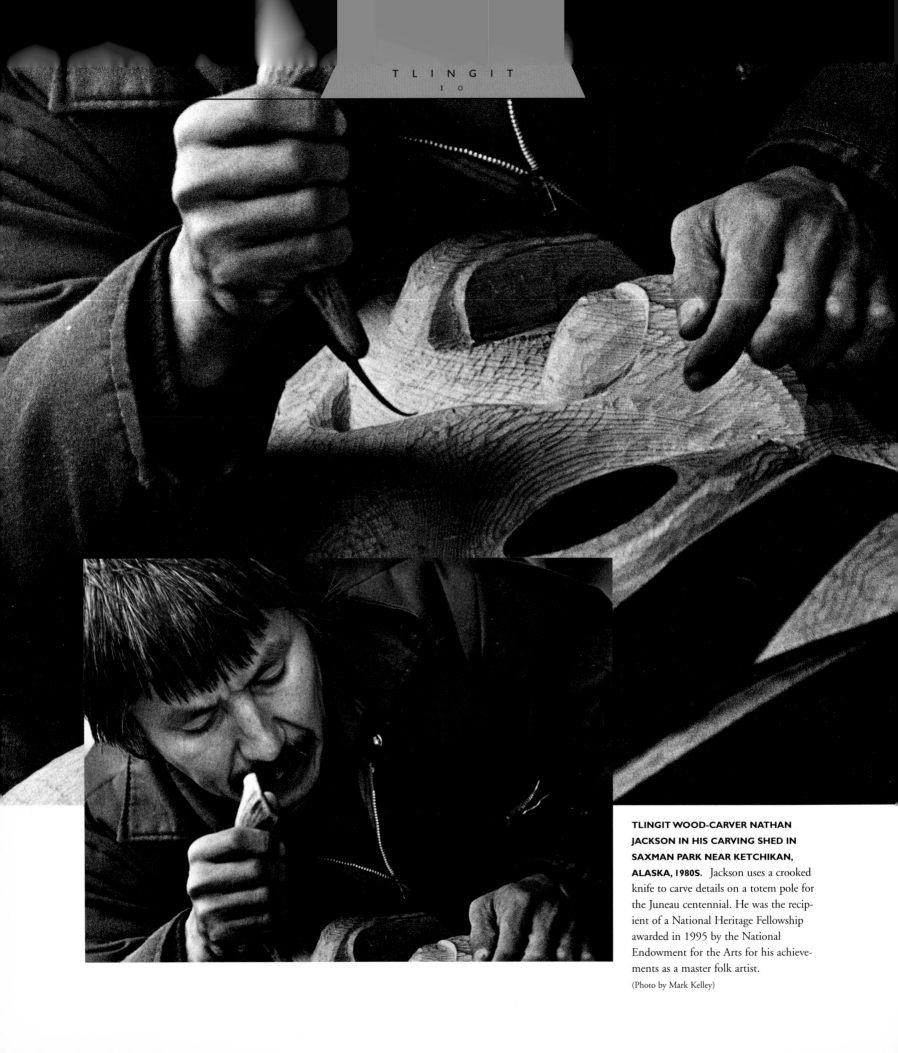

TLINGIT WOOD-CARVER NATHAN JACKSON IN HIS CARVING SHED IN SAXMAN PARK NEAR KETCHIKAN, ALASKA, 1980S. Jackson uses a crooked knife to carve details on a totem pole for the Juneau centennial. He was the recipient of a National Heritage Fellowship awarded in 1995 by the National Endowment for the Arts for his achievements as a master folk artist.

(Photo by Mark Kelley)

PAINTED STORAGE BOX
Haida, collected 1904

PAINTER'S PATTERN
Tlingit, purchased 1894

PAINTBRUSH
Chilkat Tlingit, purchased 1888

ELBOW ADZE
Tlingit, Yakutat, Alaska, pre-1970

Northwest Coast men are renowned for their tradition of wood carving and painting. They carve everything in wood, from monumental totem poles to delicate face masks.

When painting two-dimensional designs or carving in relief, northern coastal artists share a set of design principles, even though no two objects are exactly alike. Animals, particularly those representing a family or clan, are the source of the designs.

Artists might split the animal design so it wraps around a box, or they might rearrange its parts, all the while conforming to a basic set of compositional rules. They draw freehand or use cedar bark templates to trace symmetrical patterns before painting them in the preferred colors of red, black, and blue-green.

Box: Cedar?, mineral paints; H 15.8 in. (31.5 L x 33.5 W x 40.2 H cm); 3178-118

Pattern: Yellow cedar bark *(Chamaecyparis nootkatensis);* L 17.0 in. (43.2 L x 14.5 W x 1.0 H cm); 638-8

Paintbrush: Unidentified wood, Sitka spruce root *(Picea sitchensis),* porcupine hair *(Erethizon dorsatum);* L 7.3 in. (18.5 L x 1.0 D cm); 638-7

Adze: Red alder? *(Alnus rubra),* iron, steel; L 18.9 in. (48.0 L x 15.0 W x 7.2 H cm); 24386-2, gift of Dr. Oshin Agathon

MASK
Nuuchahnulth or Kwakwaka'wakw (Kwakiutl),
Kyoquot Sound or Quatsino Sound, early 1800s

CROOKED KNIFE
Chilkat Tlingit, purchased 1894

With the all-purpose crooked knife, a woodworker could carve curved surfaces and the finest details on rattles, masks, boxes, and other decorative items. This dance mask shows the tool marks of a specialist skilled in carving wood.

Mask: Unidentified wood, mineral paints, iron; L 8.7 in. (22.0 L x 16.0 W x 8.5 H cm); 3178-36. Knife: Unidentified wood, leather, steel; L 8.0 in. (20.2 L x 2.0 D cm); 638-9

COLLECTING SKUNK CABBAGE, 1912. A Salish woman collects skunk cabbage. *The big leaves are good for wrapping things—just like wax paper,* says Nora Marks Dauenhauer.[14]

(Photo by Edward S. Curtis. William R. Oliver Special Collections, Carnegie Library of Pittsburgh)

Then go out by the cool stream
and get some skunk cabbage,
because it's biodegradable,
to serve the salmon from.
Before you take back the skunk cabbage,
you can make a cup out of one
to drink from the cool stream.

NORA MARKS DAUENHAUER, TLINGIT, 1988[15]

CANOE BAILER

Southern Northwest Coast, ca. 1993

The lush forests have always stood right outside the Northwest Coast people's back doors, ready to supply their daily needs. In the past, from Frederick Sound north, the Tlingit people gathered the Sitka spruce for multiple uses. The Western red cedar, which ranges from Frederick Sound to California, supplied the needs of the southern Tlingit and their neighbors.

Every part of that tree was used. Our houses, the beams, they were all made out of the cedar tree. The boards that were on the houses, they were from this tree. The utensils we have, the canoes, there was just so much that came from this tree. And the bark, of course, was stripped during the spring, when it was easily removed. . . . And this was our clothing and our baskets and our mats and our towels. And so every part of that tree was very important for us.

DAISY SEWID-SMITH,
KWAKWAKA'WAKW, 1994[16]

Western red cedar (*Thuja plicata*), nylon; L 14.0 in. (35.6 L x 20.3 W x 18.8 H cm); 35731-1

SPRUCE ROOT HAT
Tlingit, collected 1904

Conifers cover over 50 percent of southeast Alaska. Western hemlock and Sitka spruce are the most abundant. The Sitka spruce, Alaska's state tree, grows to 225 feet in height and to 8 feet in diameter, and it can live to be 700 years old.

Tlingit women devised a technique for weaving containers and hats from the roots of the Sitka spruce tree. Both women and men wore this type of common work hat, particularly for canoe travel.

Sitka spruce root *(Picea sitchensis),* cedar?; D 17.3 in. (22.0 H x 44.0 D cm); 3178-123a

UTILITY BASKET
Nuuchahnulth, pre-1898

Open-worked baskets were used for everyday tasks such as carrying clams. Excess water drained easily from these sturdy baskets.

Western red cedar *(Thuja plicata),* commercial wool; L 12.2 in. (31.0 L x 7.5 W x 7.1 H cm); 638-18

Gifts from Trees

Native North American basketmakers selected their raw materials from readily available plants. In Alaska, women constructed their baskets from materials harvested from conifer trees—Sitka spruce tree roots and the inner bark of the Western red cedar.

Basketmakers in the Northeastern woodlands also depended on trees for their materials; however, they used logs. They pounded hardwood logs from deciduous trees until the wood separated into layers that could then be split apart and made into plaited-splint baskets.

Northeastern Native women used a range of techniques specific to their region to decorate their baskets. They twisted wood strips to create curlicues, dyed splints with bright colors, or stamped them with curvilinear designs using cutout potatoes, turnips, corks, or pieces of wood. Sweetgrass was often incorporated to give a pleasant aroma.

COVERED STORAGE BASKET

Southern New England, late 1800s

Black ash *(Fraxinus nigra)*, commercial paint; D 16.5 in. (28.0 H x 42.0 D cm); 35459-29a & b

STRAWBERRY BASKET

Penobscot, Maine, ca. 1900

Black ash *(Fraxinus nigra)*, dye, sweetgrass *(Hierochloe odorata)*; H 13.3 in. (34.0 H x 24.5 D cm); 1456-3 a & b

STAMPED BASKET

Mahican?, western Massachusetts or Connecticut, 1800-1850

Black ash *(Fraxinus nigra)*, commercial paint, paper, commercial cotton cord; L 13.4 in. (34.0 L x 24.0 W x 22.0 H cm); 35459-24

CLAN LEADERS, 1907. Three Chilkat clan leaders hold raven rattles, emblems of the men's prominence, in the correct, inverted position.
(Photo by W. H. Case and H. H. Draper. Alaska State Library, 39-443)

I talk to the bear when I'm in the woods.
When I see bear tracks
I would look at it
and I could smell it's very near.
"My paternal uncles,
I'm here in the woods to get food
for your grandchildren."

ANDREW P. JOHNSON, TLINGIT, 1975[17]

RAVEN RATTLE
Haida?, mid 1800s

Raven rattles conventionally depict a complex scene in which a human reclines on the back of a raven while his tongue connects with the tongue of a frog. Meanwhile a second bird's head, formed from the raven's tail, holds the frog. High-ranking men carried these rattles with the scene inverted as they danced ceremoniously.

Maple? *(Alcer sp.)*, mineral and commercial paints, sinew, pebbles?;
L 13.3 in. (34.0 L x 9.5 W x 9.5 H cm); 3178-2

*I talk to the bear when
I'm in the woods.*

TRANSFORMATIONS

CHIEF SHAKES AND ANOTHER CLAN LEADER WEAR BEAR DANCE COSTUMES, 1885. The man in the doorway masquerades in a complete brown bear skin. Chief Shakes wears a headdress with bear ears and a *Haliotis*-shell tunic with bear designs.
(Photo by Albert P. Niblack. Royal British Columbia Museum)

BEAR, RAVEN, AND HUMANS

A ccording to Tlingit mythology, animals were once humans who were frightened into the woods and the sea by the daylight that Raven let out of a box. Traditional Tlingits believe that people and animals are relatives who can cross into each other's worlds. Animals have the ability to appear before people in human form, just as humans can be transformed into animals in supernatural encounters. In Tlingit stories, animals and humans even marry and raise families.

Bear, the most important land animal, typifies this relationship between humans and animals. In nature, a bear behaves like a human and competes for the same resources. It can walk on its hind legs, fish for salmon, and use its dexterous paws to eat berries and nuts. When pursuing a bear, the hunter carefully carries out a special ritual, for he is killing a creature whose soul is akin to his own.

Raven also moves between the creature and human worlds, bestowing gifts yet playing tricks on humans in an extensive series of stories. He has a dual personality. As a culture hero and transformer, Raven is credited with shaping much of our world. As a trickster, he is driven to outlandish adventures by his selfishness, greed, and hunger.

RAVEN HAT

Tlingit, early to mid 1800s

In Tlingit society the raven has a different role from its mythic guise. Society is divided into two halves, or moieties, named the Ravens and the Eagles. Every Tlingit belongs to one side or the other. Within each moiety are many clans. This raven crest hat probably belonged to a clan that owned the right to display Raven in this guise.

Unidentified wood, Sitka spruce *(Picea sitchensis),* mineral paints, abalone shell *(Haliotis* sp.*),* commercial cotton, unidentified adhesive, laundry blueing, tanned hide, iron; L 24.9 in. (63.5 L x 51.0 W x 21.0 H cm); 3178-60

WOLF? MASK

Tsimshian, collected 1904

Bears and wolves look similar in Northwest Coast carvings. However, this mask probably represents a wolf, because wolves are usually carved with a more slender snout.

Unidentified wood, hair, abalone shell *(Haliotis* sp.*),* mineral paints; L 11.0 in. (28.0 L x 18.0 W x 13.2 H cm); 3178-28

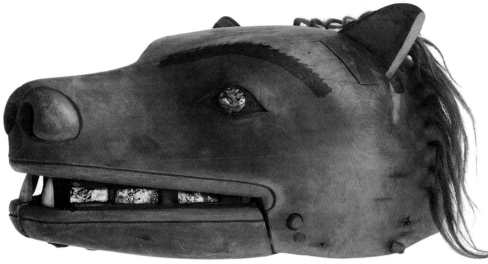

BEAR MASK

Tsimshian?, collected 1904

This mask was worn on the forehead so that the lower jaw could move like a growling bear. It was probably used by a dancer who claimed the bear as a clan or family crest.

Unidentified wood, hair, tanned hide, abalone shell *(Haliotis* sp.*)*, iron, stinging nettle *(Urtica dioica)*, unidentified bone, mineral paints, unidentified adhesive; L 13.0 in. (33.5 L x 24.0 W x 19.0 H cm); 3178-27

Tricksters

SOUTH DAKOTA

The mythological character of the trickster is widespread throughout Native North America. On the Northwest Coast, Raven is the one who plays tricks while at the same time transforming the world in useful ways. Coyote is the well-known trickster character in western America, whereas Hare goes about his mischief in the Midwest, especially in the Great Lakes region.

On the Plains, the Lakota tell stories about Spider, whom they call Iktomi.

Iktomi . . . is full of tricks, He plays his pranks on the WAKAN [spiritual beings] and on the Lakotas. When the Lakotas came from the middle of the world he would go into their lodges and then play tricks on them. He persuaded them to scatter about everywhere, and then they would be with their lodges alone, and when the enemy came upon them he would laugh at them. . . .

Iktomi is a little one. His body is like a fat bug. His legs are like the spider's, but he has hands and feet like a man. . . . He plays tricks on beasts and birds.

OLD HORSE, LAKOTA,

CA. 1900 [18]

BEADED BOTTLE

Yankton Sioux, South Dakota, collected ca. 1899

A Yankton Sioux beadworker embroidered the image of Iktomi on the hide casing of a small bottle. Since the bottle purportedly held alcohol, perhaps the spider motif gave warning about the container's contents and its potential effects on humans.

Glass, tanned hide, commercial cotton, sinew, tusk shells *(Dentalium sp.)*; H 5.5 in. (3.3 L x 10.5 W x 14 H cm.); 1171-35

To those who come asking, "Where is your history?" I answer, "We wear our history."

AUSTIN HAMMOND, TLINGIT, 1981[19]

THREE CLAN LEADERS DISPLAY CREST OBJECTS UNDER THEIR STEWARDSHIP AT RAVEN HOUSE, ANGOON, ALASKA, ABOUT 1900.

(Photo by Vincent Soboleff, Alaska State Library, 1-19)

HEIRLOOMS

CONNECTIONS WITH THE ANCESTORS

STEWARDS OF THE FAMILY HEIRLOOMS, 1900. A Chilkat couple hold crest hats at Klukwan, Alaska.

(Photo by G. T. Emmons?. Royal British Columbia Museum, PN 1782)

Crests, or emblems, of Tlingit families and clans represent creatures with whom an ancestor has interacted in the legendary past. Through purchase by the ancestor, often in exchange for his or her life, the descendants receive from the creature the right of ownership to the crest and the accompanying story, song, name, and sometimes more. Crests *don't "tell a story," but rather they allude or refer to stories already known, in much the same way a Christian cross does not "tell" the Christmas or Easter "story," but alludes to an entire spiritual tradition,* says Tlingit Nora Marks Dauenhauer.[20]

Community memory is embedded in the heirlooms that display the crests. Relatives identify with the objects through their genealogical connection. *We keep track of who has them now, of who had them in the past, and of who will have them in the future. Genealogy holds the system together,* comments Dauenhauer.[21]

NEWCOMERS

WHEN MANY CAME

Alaska's natural resources have drawn many nations to its shores. Russian, Spanish, French, British, and American explorers and fur traders all arrived in their sailing ships in the last quarter of the 1700s. At first Russia dominated the market, establishing fur-trading headquarters in southeast Alaska. Tlingit elders still tell the story of their ancestors' first meeting with white men. Except for introducing diseases, early trading encounters did not greatly interrupt traditional Tlingit life.

The United States' purchase of Alaska in 1867 brought settlers, missionaries, educators, gold prospectors, and fish canneries. This influx of outside philosophies and economic interests severely impacted Tlingit land ownership, language, culture, and self-esteem. *Whenever I speak Tlingit I can still taste the soap,* says one elder, recalling the native-language ban in the schools.[25]

Alaskan Tlingits have a unique status in the United States as a result of their historic Indian rights movement that began early in the twentieth century. They do not reside on reservations but are shareholders in their own regional corporation, Sealaska Corporation, and a dozen smaller village corporations that manage tribal lands and natural resource enterprises.

For those of us who are Tlingit, the cover will slide off from our culture. Even now our grip is weary from holding on to it.

GEORGE DAVIS, TLINGIT, 1980[26]

LAMPS
Tlingit, date unknown

Southeast Alaska became a popular tourist destination. By 1890, thousands of people each summer cruised by steamship up the waters of the Inside Passage. From the comforts of the ship, they could view the spectacular mountains and glaciers.

At various stops along the way, the visitors were met by Native vendors selling objects made specifically for tourists: basketry whimsies, model totem poles, salad forks and spoons, and other items destined for Victorian homes and tabletops. Baskets were a particular favorite among Euro-American collectors, and Tlingit women wove new forms like this pair of lamps to please this market. All these sales provided an important source of family income.

Sitka spruce root *(Picea sitchensis),* unidentified grass, glass, unidentified wood, brass, aluminum, cardboard, plastic, copper, unidentified metal alloy, dye; each H 15.7 in. (40 H x 14 D cm); 24386-4a, b, c & 5a, b, c, gift of Dr. Oshin Agathon

DANCING AND SINGING, CA. 1992.
The Mt. Fairweather Dancers and Singers
from Hoonah, Alaska, participate in the
Celebration program of the Sealaska
Heritage Foundation, a division of the
Sealaska Corporation.

*Since 1982, we the Tlingit, Haida, and
Tsimshian people of Southeast Alaska have
come together every even numbered year to
celebrate the richness of our cultures and to
honor the treasures that have been left with us
by our elders and our ancestors.*

DAVID G. KATZEEK, Founder, 1992

(Photo by Mark Kelley)

JACKET

Tlingit and Haida, Juneau, Alaska, ca. 1996

In 1912 a group of educated Tlingit and Tsimshian men founded the Alaskan Native Brotherhood (ANB) to fight for civil rights. For decades ANB leaders fought against rampant racial discrimination, finally convincing the Alaska legislature to pass the first antidiscrimination law in the nation in 1946, twenty years before the national Civil Rights movement.

The Brotherhood fought for the return of millions of acres of land that the federal government had appropriated for the Tongass National Forest. The organization's early efforts culminated in the Native Claims Settlement Act of 1971. Congress mandated the creation of the Sealaska Regional Corporation and several village corporations in southeast Alaska, conveyed lands to these corporations, and paid compensation for the remaining land claims. Today Sealaska Corporation manages thriving natural resources enterprises for its Tlingit, Haida, and Tsimshian shareholders.

The logo of the Sealaska Corporation on the back of this jacket displays the joined heads of a raven and an eagle, representing the two moieties of the Tlingit and Haida nations.

Cotton denim, copper, steel, nylon, synthetic leather, commercial dyes, ink; W 58.5 in. (64.8 L x 150.0 W cm); 36211-1, gift of Sealaska Corporation

PIPE

Haida, ca. 1900

Euro-American fur traders introduced commercial tobacco and the custom of smoking to the northern Northwest Coast Natives. The Tlingit and Haida were already cultivating native tobacco, which they mixed with lime and ash before sucking it like snuff.

Around 1821, in response to maritime trade opportunities, Haida carvers began making pipes in argillite. This soft, black stone occurs in only one vein on the Queen Charlotte Islands. The enterprising carvers produced these pipes solely to sell to sailors and shipboard passengers. Figures of Euro-American seamen intertwine with Northwest Coast sea and land creatures in these mazelike depictions.

Argillite; L 11.0 in. (28.0 L x 3.5 W x 7.5 H cm); 23102-431, gift of John A. Beck

To Hopi people, corn is life. It has sustained the people throughout their history. It is the first solid food fed to infants at their clan naming ceremony. It is also prepared for the deceased, to sustain their essences as they journey into the spirit world.

Part of the Hopi origin story recalls the time of emergence from a previous world into the present world. Those who emerged were invited to choose from a number of ears of corn. Some ears were large and hearty, indicating a life of bountifulness and material prosperity on this earth. Some were short, indicating that lessons in life would be learned from hardships but that overcoming hardships would make the people strong and enduring. Hopis chose to live the life of the short ear of corn and migrated to the lands upon which they built their enduring villages and culture.

Hartman H. Lomawaima, Hopi, 1996[1]

We are rooted in our cornfields.

In Hopi belief, if you want to teach a person the history or the song that is deeply connected to our history, you feed them corn. You're planting history into this person. Planting is really a life of Hopi.

MILLAND LOMAKEMA, HOPI, 1986[3]

CORN

CORN: AN ACT OF FAITH

Hopi people farm successfully in an arid and demanding environment. They have detailed knowledge of their environment and employ specialized agricultural methods to maximize their chances for success. Farmers select the most favorable field sites on the valley floors, generally utilizing naturally flooded areas such as the mouths of large washes to capture the runoff from heavy thunderstorms. They plant multiple seeds in each hole, resulting in clumps of plants that are wind resistant and widely spaced to prevent soil nutrient depletion. Seeds are planted twelve inches deep to take advantage of the moisture trapped in the sandy subsoil. The traditional planting dates are determined by the Sunwatcher, who observes the varying positions of the rising sun on the horizon. With the worrisome potential for both late spring and early fall killing frosts, correct timing for planting is vital. Hopi farmers increase their chances for success by making several plantings at different locations, elevations, and times.

The Hopi place high value on traditional corn horticultural techniques and continue to exert great effort in the application of these centuries-old practices, using native seeds and organic farming methods. Farming has more than economic significance. Working the corn is an act of faith.

Corn is integral to what it means to be Hopi.
Corn is basic to Hopi life.
Corn was grown and eaten by the prehistoric ancestors of the Hopi and is still considered by the Hopi as our staff of life.
In addition to its nutritional value, corn also holds symbolic value.

HARTMAN LOMAWAIMA, HOPI, 1986[4]

Hopi-grown corn is an essential element in every ceremony. Although people may supplement their supply with corn purchased from the supermarket, it is the presence of corn cultivated by the Hopi that is of primary importance.

Oh, for a heart as pure as pollen on corn blossoms
And for a life as sweet as honey gathered from the flowers,
And beautiful as butterflies in sunshine.
May I do good, as Corn has done good for my people
Through all the days that were.
Until my task is done and evening falls,
Oh, Mighty Spirit, hear my grinding song.

POLINGAYSI QOYAWAYMA, HOPI, 1964[5]

HOPI WOMAN GRINDING CORN, 1912-1922 (OPPOSITE TOP). A woman spent several hours each day grinding corn into meal for her family. She knelt at the corn-grinding bin, which held several stones ranging from coarse to fine. After grinding the kernels on the coarse stone, she would regrind the meal successively on the finer stones until she had a fine flour. She then mounded the flour firmly in a pottery bowl, ready for use. Women often worked in groups at the mealing bins, allowing them to socialize while completing the day's tasks. They created special songs, like the corn-grinding song above, to sing while grinding.

(Photo by Emry Kopta. Museum of Northern Arizona Photo Archives, MS240-2-111)

FARMER IN HIS CORNFIELD, 1912-1922. Clumping corn plants by dropping a handful of seeds into a single hole is a distinctly Hopi technique. This farmer has a healthy stand of corn, which has withstood the ravages of wind, drought, and pests.

(Photo by Emry Kopta. Collection of Mary Esther Ball Brown and John Brookens Brown)

PLANTING CORN SEEDS WITH A DIGGING STICK, 1912-1922 (FACING PAGE). Hopi farmers use a basic planting tool, the digging stick, to make the deep hole necessary to place the ten to twenty seeds at the level of moist sand. Because Hopi corn is especially adapted for deep planting, it can sprout from a twelve-inch depth.

(Photo by Emry Kopta. Museum of Northern Arizona Photo Archives, MS2808/75.870N)

CORN DRYING ON A ROOFTOP AT BACAVI VILLAGE, ABOUT 1910.
In the autumn the corn is spread out, sometimes on rooftops, to dry in the sun. The ears are then stacked like cordwood in storage areas to be used throughout the year until the next season's crop is ripe. After the dried kernels are shelled, they are boiled or ground into meal.

(Photographer unknown. Collection of Mary Esther Ball Brown and John Brookens Brown)

CORN KATSINA
AHULANI / KÄ-E TIHU
Merrel Yaira, Hopi, 1996

Tihus, commonly called *katsina* dolls, are wooden sculptures of *katsinas.* The introduction of the *tihu* with the body of an ear of corn is relatively recent. Such dolls may have a head that represents any *katsina,* thus *katsinas* and corn become linked together in this carving. *Katsina* is the Hopi preferred spelling, although *kachina* is the spelling most often found in the English literature.

Unidentified wood, commercial paint, commercial cotton cord; H 11.8 in. (30.0 H x 9.0 D cm); 36177-6

SPOTTED CORN KATSINA
AVATSHOYA TIHU
Hopi, ca. 1904

Corn *katsinas* are the most common of the plant impersonators. This *tihu* is covered with spots that represent kernels of corn.

Plant Kachinas literally bring their own water. If there is no moisture, there are no plants, and by extension should there be no plants, there will be no Hopi. Small wonder that the Corn Kachinas are so popular both in song and in dance.

BARTON WRIGHT, 1977[6]

Cottonwood (*Populus* sp.), commercial and mineral paints, commercial cotton, clay, commercial wool, unidentified feathers, juniper branch (*Juniperus communis*), horsehair (*Equus caballus*), cotton cord (*Gossypium hirsutum*), commercial dye; H 11.4 in. (16.5 W x 29.0 H cm); 3165-90

BLUE CORN MAIDEN KATSINA
SAKWAP MANA TIHU
John Fredericks, Hopi, ca. 1995

I am a naturalist, not a carver. Every piece of wood I work with already has a figure within it. I don't carve, I just bring out the form that is already there. . . . I like to do big heavy pieces. They remind me of the mesas—the mesas are wide and I feel a lot of strength from them.

JOHN FREDERICKS, HOPI, 1989[7]

Cottonwood (*Populus* sp.), commercial paint and stain; H 12.2 in. (20.0 W X 31.0 H cm); 36033-1

WEAVING COILED BASKETS, SIPAULAVI ON SECOND MESA, EARLY 1900S. Women relatives, neighbors, and friends of the bride work in a group to make basket plaques to be used to pay back the groom's family for the bridal clothing and gifts received by the bride's family.
(Photographer unknown. California Historical Society Title Insurance and Trust Photo Collection, Department of Special Collections, University of Southern California Library, 1083)

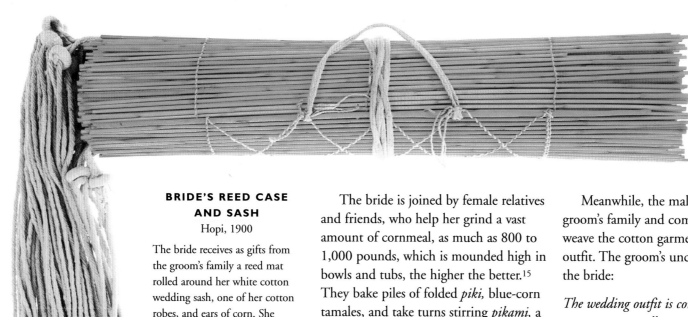

BRIDE'S REED CASE AND SASH
Hopi, 1900

The bride receives as gifts from the groom's family a reed mat rolled around her white cotton wedding sash, one of her cotton robes, and ears of corn. She carries this case of gifts in procession from her mother-in-law's house to her parents' home. Male relatives and friends of the groom's family all help to make the bridal garments.

After his breakfast, each man went to his Kiva, taking his spindle (every adult male owns one). Emory's uncle came around early to deliver to each Kiva the carded cotton to be spun. In Bacabi there were three Kivas. Soon all spindles were humming away. Emory's uncle checked the Kivas from time to time to keep them all supplied with carded cotton.

HELEN
SEKAQUAPTEWA,
HOPI, 1969 [14]

Case: Sand grass (*Calamovilfa gigantea*), cotton (*Gossypium hirsutum*); L 90.0 x W 29.3 in. (228.5 L x 74.5 W cm); 1579-14.
Sash: Cotton (*Gossypium hirsutum*), cornhusk (*Zea mays*), kaolin; L 100.4 x W 9.4 in. (255.0 L x 23.8 W cm); 1579-16

The bride is joined by female relatives and friends, who help her grind a vast amount of cornmeal, as much as 800 to 1,000 pounds, which is mounded high in bowls and tubs, the higher the better.[15] They bake piles of folded *piki,* blue-corn tamales, and take turns stirring *pikami,* a corn pudding, with a big stick in galvanized tubs. *They say no man will marry a girl unless she can make piki,* Helen Sekaquaptewa comments.[16] Women also contribute numbers of basketry trays to hold the corn gifts, which will be presented to the groom's family.

Meanwhile, the male members of the groom's family and community spin and weave the cotton garments for the bridal outfit. The groom's uncle gives a talk to the bride:

The wedding outfit is completed, and tomorrow you will return to your home. We are now the same people, sisters, brothers, uncles, and aunts to each other.

DON TALAYESVA, HOPI, 1942 [17]

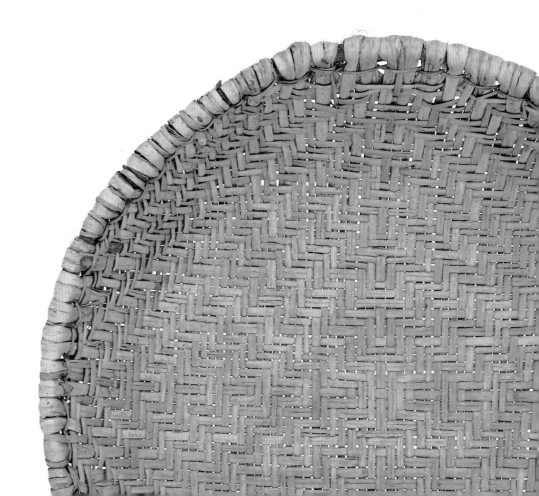

CENTRAL AND SOUTHERN CALIFORNIA

Baskets

Some of the world's finest baskets are made by Native women of North America. Basketweavers in the Southwest and California excel in this art. During the past century collectors have created a ready market for these artworks. Unfortunately, the materials needed to produce the baskets have become steadily scarcer in California as a result of urban sprawl and environmental pollution.

Weavers use techniques and forms specifically related to the function of the basket. Utility baskets are usually twined or plaited for durability and, if intended for burdens, shaped to fit on the bearer's back. Coiled trays and bowls display decorative designs that can be seen and admired while being used. Presentation baskets adorned with feathers and beads honor the esteemed recipient and are the most-admired creations among collectors.

TWINED BURDEN BASKET

Pomo, central California, ca. late 1800s or early 1900s

Willow (*Salix argophylla*), sedge root (*Carex barbarea*), redbud (*Cercis occidentalis*); H 15.0 in. (38.0 H x 38.0 D cm); 7851-204, gift of Misses Matilde and Dorothea W. Holliedt

PLAITED BASKET

Hopi, ca. 1900

The yucca sifter basket, made by women on all three Hopi mesas, is the basic utility basket. It is used for a variety of tasks—as a colander, a sifter, a winnowing tray, and a catch basin for shelling corn.

Yucca (*Yucca angustissima*), sumac (*Rhus trilobata*); D 19.7 in. (50.0 D cm); 2128-5

FEATHER PRESENTATION BASKET

Pomo, central California, ca. late 1800s or early 1900s

Sedge grass root (*Carex barbarea*), willow (*Salix argophylla*), red and yellow feathers from unidentified yellow songbird, possibly Western Meadowlark (*Sturnella neglecta*), blue feathers from Scrub Jay (*Aphelocoma californica*), California Quail black topknot feathers (*Callipepla californica*), clam shell (*Saxidomus nuttallii*), abalone shell (*Haliotis rufescens*), glass, commercial cotton thread, dye; H 5.1 in. (13.0 H x 32.0 D cm); 7851-205, gift of Misses Matilde and Dorothea W. Holliedt

COILED TRAY

Angelita Lugo, Luiseño?, Pala Reservation, southern California, ca. 1914

Deergrass (*Muhlenbergi rigens*), rush (*Juncus* sp.), sumac (*Rhus trilobata*), dye; D 19.0 in. (10.0 H x 48.2 D cm); 7851-228, gift of Misses Matilde and Dorothea W. Hollied

BRIDE'S WEDDING ROBE
Hopi, ca. 1904

A bride receives two white cotton wedding robes—one of which will someday be her burial shroud and a second that she can use communally or trade. Border stitches and tassels dangling from the robe's corners signify the bride's fertility and the future hope for children.

When the weaving was finished, the men took the robes from the looms and brought them into the house to be tried on. A border of sixteen running stitches in red was embroidered in the two corners, suggesting a limit of sixteen children, the most a person should have, and four stitches in each of the other two corners in orange, suggesting a minimum number of children.

HELEN SEKAQUAPTEWA, HOPI, 1969 [18]

Cotton (*Gossypium hirsutum*), kaolin, wool (*Ovis aries*), vegetable dye; L 47.2 x W 61.8 in. (120.0 L x 157.0 W cm); 3165-28

GROOM'S COILED BASKET
Second Mesa, Hopi, late 1800s

This coiled plaque was probably made as a replica of the gift for the groom, because the last coil was left unfinished. This practice is followed so that the groom will not meet an untimely death. The plaque is filled with *piki* or corn-meal and carried by the bride to her mother-in-law's house in return for the garments and gifts that she will receive from the groom's family. At his death the groom's spirit will sail on the plaque to the Underworld.

Yucca (*Yucca angustissima*), galleta grass (*Hilaria jamesii*), vegetable dye; D 14.2 in. (36.0 D cm); 715-21, gift of United States National Museum

GROOM'S WICKER BASKET
Third Mesa, Hopi, ca. 1904

Basket weavers at Third Mesa incorporate a special design, rectangles linked together, into the wicker plaque that they make for the groom's basket. This tray and many others would be heaped high with gifts of cornmeal.

After the feast in the bride's house, it was time for them [the bride's family] and their relatives to prepare cornmeal gifts in exchange for the wedding costumes. The bride and her relatives ground corn for many days. Little girls seven and eight years old helped with the grinding. Many heaping plaques of fine cornmeal were taken to our house—perhaps twenty bushels—to be distributed among the relatives who assisted us. This completed the wedding obligations.

DON TALAYESVA, HOPI, 1942 [19]

Rabbit brush (*Chrysothamnus naseosus*), sumac (*Rhus trilobata*), yucca (*Yucca angustissima*), vegetable dye; D 12.8 in. (32.5 D cm); 3165-67

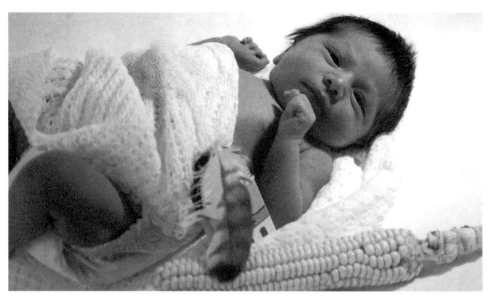

All life is a planting, a growing and a harvesting.

POLINGAYSI QOYAWAYMA,
HOPI, 1964 [20]

Children

LEARNING TO
BE HOPI

Beginning with the very first days of their lives, children are integrated into Hopi society through a number of special occasions.

I took you, newly born. I held your warm body against my bared legs. I presented you with your first Mother Corn. I pierced your little ears. For 20 days I cared for you, observing the traditional manner of caring for a newborn child. . . . it was I who named you.

PATERNAL GRANDMOTHER OF
POLINGAYSI QOYAWAYMA,
HOPI, 1964 [21]

A newborn baby spends the first nineteen days of its life secluded indoors, where it is cared for by the elder women of the family. It is wrapped in a blanket alongside one or two ears of perfectly formed corn, referred to as its Mother. On the twentieth day the baby receives its Hopi name in a sunrise naming ceremony.

As the child grows, the *katsinas* bring gifts to introduce the child to his or her lifelong pathway.

POLYCHROME CORN PUDDING BOWL
Hopi, ca. 1860-1890

This bowl held *pikami* (baked sweet cornmeal pudding) for the feast following the naming of the baby of Talaswihuonia on his twentieth day at Sipaulavi village on November 1, 1900. The two ears of Mother Corn were perfectly formed and lay nestled next to the baby for his first nineteen days.

Clay, mineral and vegetable paints; H 2.8 in. (7.2 H x 18.4 D cm); 1579-27

SKYE SEUMPTEWA WITH THE EAR OF MOTHER CORN, 1996. The baby's Hopi name is Dawa Munsi, or Sun Flower.
(Photo by Owen Seumptewa)

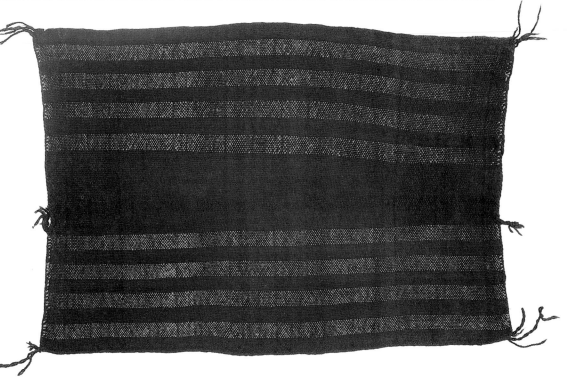

It's breathtaking when the kachinas come to the plaza to dance and sing their songs. Like at the home dance. During the afternoon, they bring bows and arrows and kachina dolls for the children. These are usually tied to long stems of deep green cattail, still moist from the distant waters. It's truly a wondrous sight, especially when the kachinas give them out after the dance. You can feel the excitement radiating from the children, and you can see the anticipation in their eyes. I remember those feelings when I was that age. Hopeful that I, too, would be befriended by a kachina who might've brought something for me. When I stand on the rooftop above the plaza watching the girls admiring their dolls—and the boys, too—it reminds me of a pond that's full of life down there, with all the cattail around the edge of the plaza, reaching up, swaying in the light breeze.

RAMSON LOMATEWAMA, HOPI, 1992[22]

Part of learning about the larger world community is learning about the katsinas. In Hopi culture, the Tihu [katsina doll] is a prayer stick and educational tool used by Hopi elders to impart knowledge and understanding about katsinas to Hopi girls.

HARTMAN LOMAWAIMA, HOPI, 1986[23]

Girls receive *tihus,* which they play with just like baby dolls, while boys receive bows and arrows. Infants still being carried by their mothers receive the flat *tihu.*

My mom told me, "I don't have any of my dolls, because we were allowed to play with them. We rolled around with them in the dirt, we played house with them, they were our babies, we role-played with them, we left them outside and they're gone." That's the purpose of these dolls. But today the dolls are carved so elaborately that people just put them on the wall.*

LEIGH JENKINS, HOPI, 1995[24]

BOY'S PLAID BLANKET
Hopi, ca. 1904

Blankets of this style are woven exclusively for males as infants, adolescents, or adults.

Boys are thought of as little birds. A boy wrapped in this one (gray and brown) is a sparrow. These are given as receiving blankets to baby boys and sometimes to boys in the family as heirlooms. Materially, these blankets are the most precious items for Hopi men.

HARTMAN LOMAWAIMA, HOPI, 1991[25]

Wool (*Ovis aries*); L 29.5 x W 19.3 in. (75.0 L x 49.0 W cm); 3165-26

KATSINA MOTHER
HAHAY'IWUUTI PUTSQATIHU
Manuel Chavarria, Hopi, 1996

All boys and girls get her as their first cradle katsina. . . . *She's got a beautiful smile on her face.*

HARTMAN LOMAWAIMA, HOPI, 1996[26]

The flat *tihu* is the type given to infants. With its red stripes, it is a prayer for growth and full development of the child.

Cottonwood (*Populus* sp.), unidentified feather, mineral paint, commercial cotton; H 8.6. in. (9.5 W x 22.0 H cm); 36177-5

Children learn lessons from the *katsinas*. The frightening giants come to teach correct social roles and behavior as they go from house to house looking for naughty children.

I saw some giantlike Katsinas (Nataskas) stalking into the village with long, black bills and big sawlike teeth. One carried a rope to lasso disobedient children. He stopped at a certain house and called for a boy. "You have been naughty," he scolded. "You fight with other children. You kill chickens. You pay no attention to the old people. We have come to get you and eat you." The boy cried and promised to behave better. . . . the boy's parents begged for his life and offered fresh meat in his place. The giant reached out his hand as if to grab the boy but took the meat instead. Placing it in his basket, he warned the boy that he would get just one more chance to change his conduct. I was frightened and got out of sight.

DON TALAYESVA, HOPI, 1942[27]

Children are expected to provide the food their parents give to the monsters in exchange for their offspring. From this experience Hopi children learn not only correct behavior but also their roles as future Hopi women and men.

To me, having had firsthand experience with these figures, the lesson I learned is that there are certain expectations placed upon Hopi men and women, and part of a child's growing and rearing is learning how to meet some of these expectations. The boys are supposed to learn something about planting, the weaving traditions, and how to care for their families by providing food and so on. And the girls need to learn to make piki and someviki, the little tamales—culinary skills—in addition to collecting herbs and medicines and so on.

These are the things that Hopi children must learn. And these giants come to see how you're progressing. They are interested in knowing how you're doing personally as well as how the teaching process is going in your home. Are your uncles or father or parents instructing you in these things? The proof is how you respond to these figures when they come to visit your house. The boys will trap mice or rats or something and give them as a kind of tribute to the giants. The girls will make miniature tamales to give to them. In addition, fathers will present some fresh lamb or mutton or whatever to these giants to indicate that, yes, they are being models for how to provide for the family.

HARTMAN LOMAWAIMA,
HOPI, 1996[28]

FOUR LITTLE GIRLS PLAY WITH THEIR *TIHUS*, WHICH THEY RECEIVED AS GIFTS FROM THE KATSINAS, 1912-1922. *It is the maternal Uncle who performs the job of kachina's aide by crafting with great love and precision the "Tihu" that the child will receive. Maternal Uncles figure prominently in the rearing and training of Hopi children and continue to serve as respected advisors well into adulthood.*

HARTMAN LOMAWAIMA,
HOPI, 1986[29]

(Photo by Emry Kopta. Museum of Northern Arizona Photo Archives, MS240-2-124)

QÖTSAWIHAZRU TIHU (LEFT)
Hopi, ca. 1904

NATA'ASKA TIHU (CENTER)
Hopi, ca. 1904

SO´YOKWUUTI TIHU (RIGHT)
Hopi, ca. 1904

The female disciplinarian, So´yokwuuti, right, comes to the house a week early to tell the children that they must prepare food for the giants' return. She gives boys a snare to catch small rodents and girls corn to grind. In her hand she is holding a staff to snatch children by the neck and on her back a basket to carry them away.

My grandfather told me how, when he was a boy, the giant female Katcina (Soyocco) entered the village and went from house to house looking for naughty children. She warned boys to behave, gave them a couple of sticks for a trap, and ordered them to catch mice. She gave girls a handful of baked sweet corn to grind into meal. Then she announced a date when she would return with the other giants for her reward of game and meal, or else the children.

DON TALAYESVA,
HOPI, 1942 [30]

The frightening giant *katsinas* come in groups to the homes of children, clacking their long beaks as they await either food or a naughty child to devour. The white giant, Wiharu, left, is quite dapper in his corduroy suit.

Nata'aska [center] is a giant, bigger than life, and, of course, when you're a five year old everybody is big, especially these. Their purpose is, in a sense, to catch your attention as a youngster, and they do that very easily. But I don't know who started calling them ogres. . . . I think it's somewhat misleading because if I were thinking about an ogre in Pittsburgh, Pennsylvania, I might be thinking of some imaginary creature that is under my bed. I've heard some of the European children's fairy tales where the term ogre *is used, but it's really something else for us.*

HARTMAN LOMAWAIMA, HOPI,
1996 [31]

Left: Cottonwood (*Populus* sp.), commercial cotton (corduroy), tanned deer? hide (*Odocoileus* sp.), cottontail? fur (*Sylvilagus* sp.), wool (*Ovis aries*), cotton (*Gossypium hirsutum*), silk, cornhusk (*Zea mays*), Prairie Falcon feathers (*Falco mexicanus*), Wild Turkey feathers (*Meleagris gallopavo*), unidentified semiplumes, commercial and mineral paints, commercial dye; H 14.6 in. (20.0 W x 37.0 H cm); 3165-104

Center: Cottonwood (*Populus* sp.), commercial cotton, tanned deer? hide (*Odocoileus* sp.), cornhusk (*Zea mays*), Mariam's Turkey feathers (*Meleagris gallopavo mariami*), Guilded Flicker feathers (*Colaptes chrysoides*), unidentified feathers, horsehair (*Equus caballus*), cotton (*Gossypium hirsutum*), sinew, mineral paint, kaolin, unidentified adhesive; H 15.7 in. (25.5 W x 40.0 H cm); 3165-320-O

Right: Cottonwood (*Populus* sp.), commercial cotton, wool (*Ovis aries*), American Crow feathers (*Corvus brachyrhynchos*), male Northern Pintail duck feathers (*Anas acuta*), unidentified feathers, horsehair (*Equus caballus*), rabbit brush (*Chrysothamnus naseosus*), tanned hide, commercial and mineral paints, commercial dye; H 10.8 in. (15.5 W x 27.5 H cm); 3165-180

Beyond CORN

BEANS, SQUASH, AND OTHER CROPS

The Hopi utilized 134 of the 150 plant species in their environment.[32]

The Hopi cultivate a variety of plants and collect wild plants for basket making, medicines, and many other uses. Yucca roots, for example, provide the ingredients for ritual hair washing.

The indigenous food crops of corn, beans, and squash were, and to some extent still are, the principal foods. Walled garden plots on the slopes of the mesas, irrigated from nearby springs, continue to yield chiles and vegetables. Cultivated crops, including corn, beans, squash, and cotton, were introduced from Mexico and Central and South America before Spanish contact.

Peaches and apricots, introduced l the Spaniards and planted in orchard provide irregular (due to frosts) but tiful crops. These are preserved by d on rooftops.

WINNOWING THE DRIED BEAN PLANTS AT THE HONANIE HOME, KYKOTSMOVI, 1980. In 1939 Alfred F. Whiting counted twenty-three varieties of beans growing at Hopi.[33] Such types as black beans, yellow beans, purple string beans, black and tan pinto beans (all *Phaseolus vulgaris*), and tepary beans (*Phaseolus acutifolius*) are cultivated using floodwater and dry-farming techniques. Beans provide a necessary protein complement to corn and are also an important dietary source for fiber and nutrients.

(Photos by Helga Teiwes. Arizona State Museum, The University of Arizona, 54176-54178)

The girls who were married last winter have to put on their wedding blanket and go out to see the dance, the last dance [of the katsina season], to show the clouds they want rain.

CROW-WING, HOPI, 1921[40]

Hopi people play an active role in bringing rain. Both as a community and as individuals, the people are responsible for attracting water, thereby turning the cycle of agriculture. When everyone comes together during the ceremonies and everything is done in the correct way, it rains. Otherwise, there is no rain.

They are having a meeting at Walpi this evening, because we are not having rain. All the chiefs are talking to the people about their way, and how they used to be. They say that they think we haven't any rain because the younger men are stopping going into the societies; nor do the boys care about the old ways.

CROW-WING, HOPI, 1921[41]

Katsinas deliver the rain to the people, but they also give much more.

The idea of bringing water, well, that's part of it but it's not the whole picture. . . . We also regard the katsinas as friends. . . . When they bring gifts—bows and arrows or produce, vegetables or whatever, to give to people—they have somebody in particular in mind. . . . Somebody behind you will invariably say, "This katsina wants to make friends with you by giving you this gift." This particular kind of katsina from that point on has become your friend, and you have become his or her friend. . . . So it's a way of keeping the whole thing together. Not only are you trying to establish good relations among your neighbors, clan members, and family, but you have an opportunity to create this perfect friendship with something that's coming from a

very different world from your own. . . . Katsinas have the powers to bring water and life to the Earth and to sustain life.

HARTMAN LOMAWAIMA, HOPI, 1996[42]

Katsinas and their representative *tihus* often wear the clouds and the rain (see pages 54-55). They may have stacks of clouds on their heads and embroidered rain falling from their colorful dance kilts. On the rain sashes each knot is a cumulus cloud from which long fringe swishes like pouring rain. Some *tihus* illustrate water in special ways, holding a lightning bolt or wearing a water board on their backs. Bull roarers, paddles on strings that the *katsinas* twirl, make a whirring sound to attract the wind. The wind in turn brings the rain. Everywhere there is the prayer for rain.

Clouds and rain are frequent motifs on all Hopi arts. Rain clouds are regularly depicted as stylized terraced triangles, often with vertical stripes of rain showering from them. Painted and sculpted birds, butterflies, flower blossoms, and the sun all represent those things that appear after a rain shower and signal a fruitful growing season.

RAIN SASH
Hopi, ca. 1904

The all-white, braided sash is called either a "rain sash" or a "big belt." Each cornhusk ring represents a cumulus cloud with the long fringe signifying falling rain.

This knotted and fringed belt forms a part of the bridal costume, which is prepared for the Hopi bride by her [groom's] relatives, while she lives in the house of her husband prior to her "going home" to the house of her parents. On that occasion, however, it is used for the first time; it is not worn by her, but *wrapped up in connection with a large robe in a reed receptacle. Later on this belt is used in ceremonies only, by men as well as by women. . . . It is always made of cotton.*

H. R. VOTH, 1904[43]

Cotton (*Gossypium hirsutum*), cornhusk (*Zea mays*), kaolin; L 102.4 x W 9.1 in. (260.0 L x 23.0 W cm); 3165-20

SALAKMANA KATSINA
Hopi, ca. 1904

The Salakmana girl, or maiden, wears lots of clouds in her headdress. On her forehead is an ear of corn, the logical outcome of the abundant rainfall she brings. On rare occasions following the Niman Ceremony, the Salakmana male and female pair will make an appearance together. This *tihu* is an unusually large and elaborate example.

Cottonwood (*Populus* sp.), unidentified wood, commercial and mineral paints, laundry blueing, Wild Turkey feathers (*Meleagris gallopavo*), unidentified large owl feathers, unidentified feathers, steel, unidentified resin, commercial dye; H 25.6 in. (57.0 W x 65.0 H cm); 3165-168 (doll), 3165-302 (headdress)

DEITY OF THE SKY
SOOTUKWNANG TIHU
Hopi, ca. 1904

[Sootukwnang, deity of the sky] appears on different special occasions [Mixed Dances] carrying a thunder board in his right hand and a lightning frame [bolt] under his left arm. As he walks through the village he occasionally twirls the thunder board.

H . R . V O T H , 1 9 0 4 [44]

The markings above his eyes represent snow clouds, and his tall, peaked headdress indicates the towering thunderclouds. The whirring sound of the thunder board, or bull roarer, attracts the wind that brings the rain.

Cottonwood (*Populus* sp.), unidentified wood, commercial and mineral paints, commercial cotton, wool (*Ovis aries*), glass, red coral, unidentified feathers, commercial dye; H 16.1 in. (12.4 W x 41.0 H cm); 3165-187

CUMULUS CLOUD KATSINA
OMAWKATSINA
Hopi, ca. 1904

Omawkatsina has towering thunderclouds with falling rain on his *tableta* (headdress) and mask.

Cottonwood (*Populus* sp.), commercial and mineral paints, unidentified songbird feathers, unidentified down feathers, laundry blueing; H 13.8 in. (13.0 W x 35.0 H cm); 3165-147

TABLETA
Hopi, ca. 1904

Hopi teen-age girls wear these headdresses in the autumn Butterfly Dance. The young ladies choose their dance partners from among their young uncles and nephews. These boys make the *tabletas* for the girls, who keep them as mementos of their youth.

On the top of this headdress are birds and sunflowers with a terraced cloud in the center. Two Sun *katsinas* flank towering clouds and falling rain. On the reverse side are sun and sunflower designs. All of these elements are associated with the summer rains.

Pine? (*Pinus* sp.), commercial and mineral paints, laundry blueing, commercial leather, tanned deer? hide (*Odocoileus* sp.), commercial cotton, unidentified large owl feathers, cotton (*Gossypium hirsutum*); 19.3 W in. (49.0 W x 44.0 H cm); 3165-301

*Some of this clay
may even contain
the dust of my
ancestors . . .
I too might become
part of a vessel, some
day! What a
thought.*

AL QOYAWAYMA, HOPI, 1987[45]

Pottery

WHEN THE
WATER COMES

*All the water used, except
what can be caught from
melting snow in winter and
from rains during the two
rainy months of summer in a
few small holes on the mesa
top, must be carried up the
mesa on the backs of the
women in jugs holding
about three gallons. This is
the hardest thing in the life
of a Hopi woman.*

J. G. OWENS, 1892[46]

auling water was one of the major daily tasks in the life of a Hopi family. Women carried water in large, globular pottery canteens that they transported in cloth burdens slung over their backs. Hopi women preferred this method to balancing pottery jars on their heads as the women at Acoma and Zuni did. When metal buckets became available, the Hopi were quick to appreciate their light weight and durability.

*A Taos girl, when asked what she wanted
for a wedding present, answered: "A
bucket."*

ERNA FERGUSSON, 1940[47]

Hopi people were ever prepared to utilize the rains that came in July and August. Women collected water from hollowed-out cisterns on the mesa top or from springs at the base of the mesa. They stored the water in canteens or poured it into larger pottery jars at home. Today many of the mesa-top villages are still without running water.

**A HOPI WOMAN IRRIGATES HER GARDEN WITH
HER POTTERY CANTEEN, 1912-1922.**

(Photo by Emry Kopta. Museum of Northern Arizona Photo
Archives, MS240-2-550)

*As I climb over the mesas and through the
washes looking for clay, I realize that there
have been many before me who have taken
the same steps and have made the same
search—and have seen the same beauty. I
know that some of this clay may even contain the dust of my ancestors—so—how
respectful I must be. And I think, perhaps
I too might become part of a vessel, some
day! What a thought.*

AL QOYAWAYMA, HOPI, 1987[48]

HOPI GIRLS AT A SPRING, 1906.
(Photo by Edward S. Curtis. William R. Oliver Special
Collections, Carnegie Library of Pittsburgh)

**HOPI WOMEN CARRYING
WATER FROM THE VALLEY
TO THE MESA-TOP VILLAGE
OF MISHONGNOVI, ABOUT
1900** (OPPOSITE BOTTOM).
(Photographer unknown. California
Historical Society Title Insurance and
Trust Photo Collection, Department
of Special Collections, University of
Southern California Library, 4607)

BIRCH-BARK BOWL
Anishinabe, western Great Lakes,
date unknown

Birch bark (*Betula papyrifera*), spruce root
(*Picea* sp.), ash (*Fraxinus* sp.); L 10.3 in.
(26.1 L x 16.5 W x 14.8 H cm); Z-9-234

Containers

GREAT LAKES, MIDWEST, AND SOUTHWEST

HIDE PAIL
Arapaho,
Oklahoma, ca. 1903

Cow scrotum (*Bos
taurus*), paint, rawhide,
tanned hide, tinned
metal, sinew; L 8.3 in.
(21.0 L x 15.0 D cm);
3179-233

All cultures devise containers to hold, transport, and cook liquids. These receptacles reveal information about the environment of the people who made them. In the Southwest, Native Americans coiled clay into pottery containers. On the Plains they made vessels from game animal parts, such as the stomach and the scrotum. People from the West Coast wove watertight baskets, whereas those from the Great Lakes region made containers from bark peeled from trees.

CANTEEN
Hopi, ca. 1900

A smallpox epidemic
following upon a drought
and famine caused
numerous Hopi families to
flee to Zuni Pueblo in the
1860s, where they
remained for several years.
When they finally returned
home, Hopi potters
brought with them Zuni
pottery designs, which they
applied to their own
pottery. The painted scrolls
on this canteen may be
stylized "rain bird" motifs.

Clay, mineral paints; L 11.0 in.
(28.0 L x 25.0 W x 21.0 H
cm); 1946-59

POTTERY JAR
Tohono O'odham, Arizona, pre-1955

Clay, unidentified plant fiber, paint; H 13.0
in. (33.0 H x 33.0 D cm); 17212-13, gift of
Mrs. Rosalie G. Sheedy

COOKING BASKET
Hupa, northern California, pre-1932

Hazel (*Corylus rostrata californica*), conifer root, beargrass
(*xerophyllum tenax*); H 9.6 in. (24.5 H x 33.0 D cm); 9331-61,
gift of Mrs. Thomas R. Hartley

JUA FENCE CREW
Regina Naha, Hopi, 1991

For over a century the Hopi have been embroiled in a struggle with the Navajo nation and the United States government to maintain their traditional land base. The roots of this conflict began in 1882 when President Arthur established a reservation for the "Hopi and other such Indians" within the boundaries of the large Navajo Reservation. As the population of the Navajo grew, they began to occupy most of the territory, including Hopi land. The court established the Joint Use Area (JUA) in 1962, and in 1974 the JUA was partitioned into two areas— one exclusively for the Hopi, the other for the Navajo. Those families finding themselves on the wrong side of the fence were ordered to relocate to the other side.

Regina Naha's carving records this event and its dispute. In 1996 President William Clinton signed legislation designed to end the century-old disagreement. This new law stipulates that the Navajo families may remain on Hopi land under a seventy-five-year lease. In return the U.S. government will compensate the Hopi tribe with a payment that will likely be used to purchase 500,000 acres of trust land in northern Arizona to add to its reservation.

Cottonwood (*Populus* sp.), commercial paints, metal? wire, felt; H 8.3 in. (20.0 L x 13.5 W x 21.0 H cm); 35154-1

"DON'T WORRY, BE HOPI" T-SHIRT
Janice Q. Day, Second Mesa, Hopi, 1988

Janice Q. Day cleverly originated this humorous variation of the popular song title "Don't Worry, Be Happy," recorded by Bobby McFerrin in 1988. Hopi people enjoy wearing these amusing shirts and give them as gifts to their friends and relatives.

Commercial cotton, ink, chemical/commercial dye; L 33.0 in. (84.0 L x 98.0 W cm); 35568-1

NORTH | SOUTH | EAST | WEST

The Iroquois Nations of the Northeast

AND THIS IS WHAT HE HIMSELF DID, HE WHO IN THE SKY DWELLS, OUR CREATOR. . . . HE DECIDED, "I WILL CREATE A WORLD BELOW THE SKY WORLD. AND THERE THEY WILL MOVE ABOUT, THE PEOPLE I CREATE ON THE EARTH. AND THERE IS A WAY PEOPLE WILL HAVE TO REFER TO IT AS RELATED, THIS IS THE EARTH: 'OUR MOTHER, IT IS RELATED TO US, THAT WHICH SUPPORTS OUR FEET.' "

ENOS WILLIAMS, MOHAWK,
TURTLE CLAN, 1970[1]

KI-ON-TWOG-KY or CORN PLANT

A SENECA CHIEF.

PUBLISHED BY E. C. BIDDLE, PHILADELPHIA.

Printed & Coloured at I.T.Bowen's Lithographic Establishment No. 94 Walnut St.

Entered according to act of Congress in the Year 1837 by E.C.Biddle, in the Clerks Office of the District Court of the Eastern District of Penn.

We trace our ancestry in this land [to] many, many thousands of years ago. And we were created as distinct national entities when the Confederacy was formed by our Peacemaker. We are free people. We are sovereign people. We have our own nation governments. We have a distinct culture. We have a specific land base. We have a specific language. We fit the international definition of sovereign peoples.

DOUG GEORGE, MOHAWK, 1998[2]

ANCESTRY IN THE LAND

From the sixteenth century on, six nations have allied themselves to form the Iroquois Confederacy. They call themselves Haudenosaunee, the People of the Longhouse. The Mohawk nation has historically stood guard at the easternmost door of the symbolic longhouse in New York State. The Seneca watch over the western door, while the other member nations, the Oneida, Onondaga, Cayuga, and the Tuscarora (who joined in 1722-1723), are spread in between.

Sovereign PEOPLE

Cornplanter, the renowned Seneca war chief and leader, was personally given a grant of land along the Allegheny River in 1791 by the grateful Commonwealth of Pennsylvania. His assistance in keeping the Seneca neutral during the Indian Wars in Ohio helped to earn him this reward.

Cornplanter's Grant was not really a reservation, since the land was a gift to him as an individual. Because of its geographic location, wedged between the banks of the river and the mountains, the grant offered a measure of asylum and insulation from the pressures of a new expanding nation. Here the Seneca people could continue to plant, hunt, and live their traditional lives.

In 1798 four hundred Seneca (one-fourth of their total population) lived within the grant at the town of Burnt House, also known as Jenuchshadego. Many were major figures in the Iroquois Confederacy. Noted residents included Cornplanter himself; his half brother, the prophet Handsome Lake; his uncle Guyasuta; his nephew "Governor" Blacksnake; and Blacksnake's sister, who was the matron of the Wolf clan and the leading woman of the community.

While Handsome Lake lived at Cornplanter's Grant, he founded a new religion that emphasized a revitalization of the traditional seasonal ceremonies, a strengthening of the family, and a prohibition against liquor. His teachings were based on a series of visions. Since the Iroquois believed that dreams were an important instrument for revelations, Handsome Lake's visions were received as divine prophecies.

After Handsome Lake's death in 1815, his teachings continued to spread and became the foundation for the Longhouse religion. Still a vital force, this religion plays an important role in preserving the Iroquois' sacred and cultural heritage.

CORNPLANTER (CA. 1740-1836)
E. C. Biddle, northeastern United States, 1837

FRAGMENT FROM CORNPLANTER'S CABIN
Seneca, collected by Cornplanter's grandson in 1908

During the American Revolution, an Iroquois warrior arose to prominence, becoming a principal Seneca leader. He was called Cornplanter but was also known as John O'Bail after his Dutch trader father.

After the Revolution, Cornplanter quickly determined that keeping the peace with the Euro-Americans was the best way to help his own people. Though his mission as a peacekeeper was often unpopular and difficult, he negotiated the best possible terms for his people on numerous occasions when he traveled to Philadelphia as a statesman.

Cornplanter's portrait was painted in 1796 by F. Bartoli in New York City. Later this lithograph, based on the oil painting, was published in *The History of the Indian Tribes of North America,* a multivolume work by McKenney and Hall.

Lithograph: Paper, ink, paint; L 19.7 in. (50.5 L x 36.5 W cm); 36026-1. Cabin fragment: Eastern white pine (*Pinus strobus*), paper, ink, adhesive; L 9.1 in. (23.5 L x 11.7 W x 2.5 H cm); 3641-8, gift of G. M. Lehman

HANDSOME LAKE PREACHING. In 1799, Handsome Lake had the first of several visions while deathly ill. A messenger from the Creator appeared to tell him what the Creator wanted of the Iroquois. Handsome Lake preached these messages to the Cornplanter Senecas and to other Seneca settlements in what became known as the Code of Handsome Lake.

(Watercolor by Ernest Smith, Seneca, 1936. Rochester Museum and Science Center, Rochester, New York, MR707)

The Iroquois have always patterned their lives according to the seasons of the year, which give clues to appropriate activities tied to the environment. The people gave names to each new moon according to seasonal events, for example, Maple Moon, Planting Moon, Corn Harvest Moon, and Moon of Falling Leaves.

The change of seasons continues to be especially meaningful for those Iroquois who follow the Longhouse religion. Seasonal celebrations, such as the Strawberry, Green Corn, and Harvest Ceremonies, emphasize thankfulness for what has been provided in each season. *We do not ask as you whites do; we give thanks,* says an Iroquois ritualist.[3]

Today, unfortunately, Cornplanter's Grant is underwater. In 1965 the United States Army Corps of Engineers completed Kinzua Dam, inundating all of the habitable land of Cornplanter's Grant, plus 10,000 acres of the Seneca's Allegany Reservation in New York.

Cornplanter's descendants and the Allegany Senecas fought to halt the construction of the dam. The Senecas cited the Canandaigua Treaty of 1794, the oldest active treaty in the United States. This agreement, signed by both George Washington's representative and Cornplanter, guaranteed that the United States would never take this land. Article III states:

Now the United States acknowledges all the land within the aforementioned boundaries, to be the property of the Seneca Nation, and the United States will never claim the same, nor disturb the Seneca Nation.

The United States, however, confiscated the Seneca's land by the right of eminent domain. This decision was upheld by the United States Supreme Court. One judge, Circuit Justice Moore, expressed his dissenting opinion in 1964, citing *Great Nations, like great men, should keep their word.*[4]

We know that that treaty is still being recognized because every year in the fall . . . we are sent treaty cloth. And that treaty cloth has gone from a calico . . . to a cheap muslin. . . . Our clan mothers say, "We don't care if it gets down to the size of a postage stamp; . . . the principle is that you are still giving us that cloth because you recognize that this treaty is still in place."

G. PETER JEMISON, SENECA, 1998[5]

CORNPLANTER'S GRANT. This scale model of the settlement of Burnt House at Cornplanter's Grant shows the four seasons and the activities that occurred in each. In 1800, four hundred Seneca lived in Burnt House in thirty log cabins scattered near the river. How do we know the details of life at the grant? How do we know, for example, how many cabins were there and what their dimensions were? How do we know that there were three horses, fourteen cows, two oxen, and twelve pigs? The detailed journals kept by Quakers whom Cornplanter invited to teach the children have provided the background for this model.

(Model by Charles F. Rakiecz, Jr., 1997. Alcoa Foundation Hall of American Indians, Carnegie Museum of Natural History.)

DETAILS FROM THE MODEL OF CORNPLANTER'S GRANT (CLOCKWISE FROM LEFT): **PICKING STRAWBERRIES IN THE SPRING, MEN PLAYING WITH SNOW SNAKES IN THE WINTER, QUAKERS TEACHING CHILDREN IN THE SUMMER.**

The THREE SISTERS

SUSTAINERS OF IROQUOIS LIFE

CORN-WASHING BASKET

Cecilia Sunday (1919-), St. Regis, Quebec, Mohawk, 1993

Among the Iroquois, the most common way to prepare corn is to make hominy. First the kernels are boiled in water mixed with hardwood ashes to loosen the hulls. Then they are dunked up and down in water in a special washing basket until the loosened hulls and ashes finally float free. The sieve-like base and tightly woven sides allow the water to drain from the bottom while the corn remains in the basket.

Black ash (*Fraxinus nigra*); L 12.2 in. (31.0 L x 28.3 W x 25.7 H cm); 35654-1

To the Iroquois people corn, beans, and squash are the Three Sisters, the physical and spiritual sustainers of life. These life-supporting plants were given to the people when all three miraculously sprouted from the body of Sky Woman's daughter.

A woman gave the Three Sisters to the people, and the plants are named for women. It is the women who have always planted, cultivated, harvested, and processed the crops.

The planting and the gardening were a privilege. They were connected to the Mother Earth, and the feeling, I was always told, was that you give birth, you plant seeds, and, because you are connected to the Mother Earth, things will grow well, things will grow bountiful.

AUDREY SHENANDOAH, DEER CLAN MOTHER, ONONDAGA, 1998[6]

Iroquois women have always had roles of great responsibility and power.

We are a matrilineal society. I trace my lineage as a Seneca through my mother. It's because my mother's Seneca and my mother's mother was Seneca; therefore, I am Seneca. And my mother's a Heron [clan]. Therefore, I'm a Heron. We go on our mother's side.

At the head of every clan is a woman. She's a clan mother. . . . It's the clan mother who is the chief counselor to the chief. She's the one who informs him and tries to keep him working in the best interests of the people.

G. PETER JEMISON, SENECA, 1998[7]

To this day the clan mothers select the male council members, or chiefs, and have veto power over the men's decisions. *But I've never seen that power exercised in my lifetime,* reflects Ron LaFrance (Mohawk, 1994).[8]

CORN

In the past Iroquois women raised several varieties of corn, including flint, flour, pod, popcorn, and sweet corn, in a range of colors. The first sound heard in the village each morning was women rhythmically pounding corn. They used large oak mortars with long, hardwood pestles. Even though corn required extensive processing, the women could have corn bread ready for dinner within two hours of removing it from the cob.

Every part of the ear of corn was used. Women braided the husks for rope and twine and coiled them into containers and mats. Shredded husks made good kindling and filling for pillows and mattresses. The corncobs served as bottle stoppers, scrubbing brushes, and fuel for smoking meat. Corn silks made hair for cornhusk dolls. Many women still make cornhusk products.

Today corn continues to be an important part of Iroquois life. Many families have small gardens where they cultivate enough white corn for their needs. A few families raise surplus corn for ceremonial use. Everyone still looks forward to the day when a good cook hangs out her sign "Corn Soup Today."

We are thanking her [Mother Earth] for giving us life just as we are life-givers.

JOANNE SHENANDOAH, MOHAWK, 1998[9]

We return thanks to the Three Sisters . . . the main supporters of our lives.

THANKSGIVING ADDRESS, SENECA, 1846[10]

PREPARING CORN, ABOUT 1910. A woman prepares corn for cooking by scraping it from the cob.
(Photographer and date unknown. Rochester Museum and Science Center, Rochester, New York, RM 2185)

THREE WOMEN HOE IN CORNFIELD.

(Watercolor by Ernest Smith, 1940. Rochester Museum and Science Center, Rochester, New York, MR 1134)

A WAY OF PLANTING

The Iroquois agricultural system was based on the hill-planting method. Women placed several kernels of corn in a hole. As the small seedlings began to grow, the farmers returned periodically to mound the soil around the young plants, ultimately creating a hill one foot high and two feet wide. The hills were arranged in rows about a pace apart.

Iroquois women mixed their crops, using a system called "interplanting." Two or three weeks after the corn was planted, the women returned to plant bean seeds in the same hills. The beans contributed nitrogen to the soil, and the cornstalks served as the bean poles. Between the rows the farmers cultivated a low-growing crop such as squash or pumpkins, the leaves of which shaded the ground thus preserving moisture and inhibiting weed growth.

The domain of women was really the area of the village itself. The homes belonged to the women, although the men were the builders and the repairmen. And the gardens and the fields were also the responsibility of the women. They took care of those foods. They spent the time that it took to plant, to weed, to tend, and to harvest them and to put them [the foods] away for storage. And, of course, they were involved in the cooking of it [the produce].

G. PETER JEMISON, SENECA, 1998[11]

CORNHUSK DOLL POUNDING CORN

Robin Bucktooth, Nedrow, New York, Onondaga, 1993

Cornhusk (*Zea mays*), commercial cotton, unidentified wood, glass, plastic, unidentified bone, commercial leather, Mourning Dove feather (*Zenaida macroura*), unidentified shell; H 11.6 in. (15.6 L x 8.4 W x 29.6 H cm); 35564-1 a-c

Preparing Food

Traditionally, gathering and preparing food have been primary tasks of Native American women. Although staple foods vary depending on the people and the region, most foods need to be processed in some way.

Horticulturalists who cultivate corn, like the Iroquois and the Pueblo peoples, must pulverize the kernels into meal before cooking a variety of dishes. Iroquois women use tall wooden mortars with four-foot-long pestles to pound corn (see page 73), whereas Pueblo women for centuries have used flat stone metates with hand-sized manos to grind their corn.

Chemehuevi and Paiute women gather wild mesquite beans and piñon nuts, which they pound in heavy-duty wooden mortars. Hupa and other California Indian women go through an ambitious series of steps to process wild acorn nuts into usable flour. Because the acorns require heavy pounding, the women place a basketry hopper with a hole in its bottom over the stone mortar like a collar. This prevents the acorn bits from scattering everywhere as the women forcefully pound the nuts into meal.

WESTERN AND SOUTHWESTERN STATES

METATE AND MANO

Four Corners region, New Mexico, Colorado, Utah, and Arizona, pre-1540

Top: Mano: Sandstone; L 7.5 in. (19.5 L x 11.2 W x 5.0 H cm); 76-374a. Bottom: Metate: Sandstone; L 17.0 in. (43.2 L x 26.2 W x 4.6 H cm); 76-374.

MORTAR

Chemehuevi, southern California, collected 1902

PESTLE

Paiute, Great Basin, western United States, pre-1904

Mortar: Unidentified wood; H 18.8 in. (36.0 D x 48.0 H cm); 1970. Pestle: Basalt; L 11.3 in. (28.8 L x 6.0 W x 5.4 H cm); 2419-24

HOPPER

Hupa?, northern California, pre-1910

Hazel (*Corylus cornuta californica*), conifer root, beargrass; (*Xerophyllum tenax*), tanned hide, hemp? (*Apocynum cannibinum*), sinew?; D 15.4 in. (14.5 H x 39.5 D cm); 8220-81, gift of Mrs. Joel W. Burdick

ANIMALS AND MEN

CLAN ANIMALS ON THE TURTLE'S BACK

Wayne Skye (1949-), Six Nations Reserve, Ontario, Canada, Wolf clan, Cayuga, 1996

The nine clan animals of the Cayuga nation stand on the great turtle's back. Clockwise from the turtle's head, they are hawk, snipe, wolf, beaver, turtle, eel, deer, heron, and bear (center). The turtle plays a large part in the Iroquois story of the Earth's origin. Long ago, according to the story, Sky Woman fell through a hole in the sky, down toward the vast waters below. The birds flew and caught her on their wings, but there was no place below for her to land. The turtle offered to support a world on his back, and the muskrat succeeded in bringing from the bottom of the sea some mud that he placed on the turtle's back. When Sky Woman landed, the Earth was ready for her on the back of the great turtle.

Moose antler (*Alces alces*), steel, adhesive; L 12.2 in. (31.0 L x 24.0 W x 14.5 H cm); 36182-1

In the FOREST

I was born a member of the Wolf clan, just like my mother and my grandmother.

KAWENNIIOSTA BOOTS, ONONDAGA, 1995 [13]

The Iroquois people organize themselves according to the model of the animal world. Everyone belongs to the clan of his or her mother, and every clan is named for an animal. Although members take their clan animal as their emblem, they do not believe that clans are descended from that animal.

Three basic clans—bear, turtle, and wolf—exist at each of the Iroquois nations. The number of additional clans varies depending upon the nation. The Mohawks have only three original clans; the Onondaga have nine.

One of the main functions of the clan is to provide kinship with clan members in other villages. For Iroquois men, who historically traveled away from home, food and lodging always awaited them in the home of another clan member regardless of how far away it was.

Most of the Iroquois men's work took place beyond the cleared home area. They spent much of their time and energy hunting, fishing, protecting their village and territory, and trading for goods.

Men made their major contribution to their families' subsistence by hunting. Their most important quarry was the deer, and they needed to shoot one a week to provide sufficient meat for their families. Hunters also stalked the black bear, sometimes traveling on snowshoes in winter or using trained dogs.

The Iroquois people tell a story about a family of brothers who chased a great bear into the sky during a hunt. There the bear became the pan of the Big Dipper and the hunters and their trained dog the handle. Each autumn since that time, the constellation turns upside down, signaling that one of the hunters has killed the bear. The bear's blood and fat fall from the sky, turning the leaves of the trees to red, orange, and yellow.

EZRA, HARRY, AND DOUGLAS JACOBS FISHING AT CORNPLANTER'S GRANT, PENNSYLVANIA. The abundant waterways of New York and Pennsylvania provided white and yellow bass, walleye, shovelnose sturgeon, and brook trout, among other species. (Photographer and date unknown. Warren County Historical Society, Miscellaneous Indian Photographs Folder)

POWDER FLASK (LEFT)
Anishinabe (Chippewa), early 1800s

POWDER HORN AND SHOT BAG (RIGHT)
Northeastern United States, ca. 1820s

Flask: Dog hide (*Canis familiaris*), unidentified wood, sinew, commercial cotton; L 7.5 in. (19.5 L x 10.0 W x 5.0 H cm.); 23102-16942, gift of John A. Beck

Horn and bag: Commercial leather, cattle horn (*Bos taurus*), unidentified wood, commercial cotton and linen, steel; horn: L 10.2 in. (26.0 L x 5.5 D cm); bag: W 11.9 in. (18.5 L x 30.5 W x 6.0 H cm); 6569-5 a & b, gift of Herman B. Hogg

The European desire for furs, especially beaver, began to dominate Iroquois affairs in the seventeenth and eighteenth centuries. In exchange for furs, Iroquois men brought home a wealth of useful trade goods, especially metal items such as guns, axes, knives, hoes, cooking pots, needles, scissors, and nails. By 1800 the Iroquois had exhausted their own supply of beaver. Through alliances, first with the Dutch and then with the English, the Iroquois established themselves as the middlemen in the fur trade. They regulated the flow of furs coming from the western tribes to the traders in the east.

THE DUTCH TRADER.

(Watercolor by Ernest Smith, Seneca. Rochester Museum and Science Center, Rochester, New York, MR 1117)

BEAVER TOP HAT
Smedley Brothers, Philadelphia, Pennsylvania.
1820-1839

In 1624, during the very first season of settlement in New York, the Dutch shipped 1,500 beaver and 500 otter skins to Europe. They were joining the fur trade that had begun one hundred years earlier to satisfy fashion-conscious Europeans. This high demand for furs was fast leading to the depletion of these animals.

Beaver felt hats were the rage in Europe and America for two centuries. The top hat was introduced in the 1780s and ultimately became part of the daily attire for men on both sides of the Atlantic.

Beaver fur felt (*Castor canadensis*), commercial leather, paper, commercial silk, ink; L 14.6 in. (37.5 L x 34.0 W x 17.5 H cm); 7677, gift of Sam Hugh Brockmier

PIPE TOMAHAWK
Northeastern United States, ca. 1811

The pipe tomahawk is an unusual combination of weapon and smoking pipe developed by Euro-Americans for trade with Native people. Iroquois men traded their furs for these popular tomahawks. Ornate examples were presented at treaty signings as diplomatic gifts to Indian leaders, who carried them as a sign of their prestige.

Unidentified wood, pewter, brass; L 20.0 in. (51.0 L x 2.5 W x 16.5 H cm); 23102-1199, gift of John A. Beck

SNOWSHOES
Chief Stanislaus Dana, Pleasant Point, Maine, Passamaquoddy, 1910

An [Iroquois] Indian can walk as fast on snowshoes as on smooth ground, and they all assure me that they can walk faster because of the long steps they are obliged to take for the shoes to pass over each other alternately. Nic [Parker] says he can walk fifty miles in a day on snowshoes. They are of great use in hunting bear, as they can overtake him with perfect ease on snowshoes the bear falling through the crust.

LEWIS HENRY MORGAN,
1849 [14]

Black ash (*Fraxinus nigra*), rawhide, commercial wool, copper, steel; L 43.4 in. (110.5 L x 34.5 W x 3.0 H cm); 33346-48 a & b, gift of Dr. James B. Richardson III

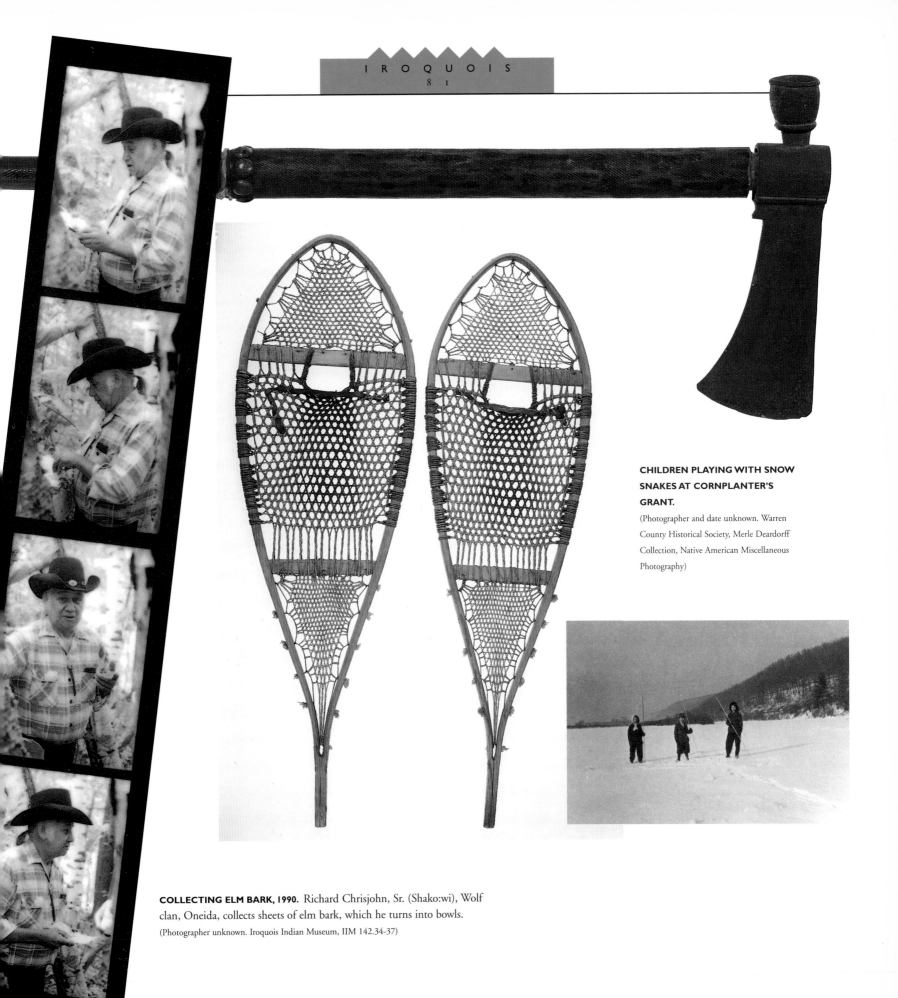

CHILDREN PLAYING WITH SNOW SNAKES AT CORNPLANTER'S GRANT.
(Photographer and date unknown. Warren County Historical Society, Merle Deardorff Collection, Native American Miscellaneous Photography)

COLLECTING ELM BARK, 1990. Richard Chrisjohn, Sr. (Shako:wi), Wolf clan, Oneida, collects sheets of elm bark, which he turns into bowls.
(Photographer unknown. Iroquois Indian Museum, IIM 142.34-37)

GEO. BARKER, PHOTOGRAPHER.

NIAGARA FALLS, NEW YORK.

506—Indian Girl—Goat Island.

Surviving CREATIVELY

A NEW ART FORM

I really wish I could have seen these falls, this set of rapids, this gorge, the way the ancestors saw it—just to hear the soothing roar and the quieting thunder that you hear. . . . You listen to them in the right way, these are going to be songs—it's going to be nature singing to you.

DuWayne Bowen, Seneca, 1996[15]

n the nineteenth century the Iroquois searched for alternative sources of income. A diminishing land base and the depletion of game and fur-bearing animals left the people with very few opportunities for earning a living. Iroquois women began to produce arts made for non-Native people. They sold their products at resorts and tourist attractions to the ever-increasing numbers of visitors.

Niagara Falls was the first and foremost American tourist attraction. European and American tourists of all ages, particularly honeymooners, flocked to see the spectacle of the falls. After the War of 1812, Tuscarora women were granted the exclusive rights to sell their beadwork at Niagara Falls by the family who owned the land on the American side. The Porter family made this offer in gratitude for the Tuscarora's service during the war and for their valor in saving the life of a Porter family member.

For well over one hundred years, tourists to the falls and area resorts purchased souvenirs from Iroquois women to take home as gifts and reminders of their trips. By the mid-nineteenth century the arts had become a major economic activity for the Iroquois and their neighboring Northeastern tribes. The women's earnings played a major role in their families' survival.

The Victorian tastes of the tourists determined the types of items the artists made and how they made them. Many of the novelties were destined for the cozy corners that were popular in Victorian homes. With ingenuity Native women produced objects that delighted female tourists interested in purchasing clothing accessories, sewing sets, and household decorations suited to the Victorian lifestyle. Many examples shown here demonstrate the cycle of exchange from Euro-American proto-types to Native artists and back to the Euro-Americans as artistic products.

Today the Iroquois look at these art forms as a part of their artistic traditions. What may once have been considered art for a white market is now regarded as an expression of Native identity and a source of pride.

Just try telling Matilda Hill that her "fancies" are tourist curios. The Tuscarora have been able to trade pieces like that bird or that beaded frame at Niagara since the end of the War of 1812, when they were granted exclusive rights, and she wouldn't take kindly to anyone slighting her culture.

RICHARD HILL,
TUSCARORA/MOHAWK, 1982[16]

ARTS FOR SALE, 1865-1875 (FACING PAGE). An Iroquois woman displays her arts for sale on Goat Island near Niagara Falls, New York.
(Photo by George Barker. Carnegie Museum of Natural History, 35068-198)

A COZY CORNER. Victorian households cluttered these special areas in their drawing rooms with souvenirs collected from around the globe.
(Photographer and date unknown. Carnegie Museum of Natural History, 35068-199)

BAG
Iroquois?, 1842

A handwritten note inside this bag reads: *A token of love to dearest Eliza Joyner from her ever affectionate sister, Harriet Howells, Feby 18th 1842, Indian Work.*

Commercial silk and cotton, glass, paper, ink; W 6.7 in. (17.0 L x 17.5 W cm); 35460-3

**NIAGARA FALLS SOUVENIRS
(CLOCKWISE FROM LEFT)**

PINCUSHION
Tuscarora?, 1870-1890

HEART PINCUSHION
Tuscarora?, 1870-1890

BAG
Tuscarora?, 1870-1890

NEEDLE CASE
Tuscarora?, 1870-1890

BOOT PINCUSHION
Tuscarora?, 1870-1890

Iroquois beaded objects far outnumber the other types of Native items made for sale. The majority were made by Tuscarora and Mohawk, especially Kahnawake (Caughnawaga), women beadworkers. Niagara Falls was the most important marketplace.

The Iroquois style of beadwork for Victorian items is unmistakable. Large translucent glass beads are clustered together to form ornate, raised patterns, usually of flowers, on dark velvet or red wool.

(Clockwise from left) Pincushion: Commercial cotton, sawdust stuffing, glass, paper; L 7.8 in. (20.0 L x 17.0 W x 7.5 H cm); 35068-164, gift of Dr. James B. Richardson III

Heart pincushion: Commercial wool and cotton, sawdust stuffing, glass, commercial silk, paper; L 4.8 in. (11.5 L x 12.5 W x 3.5 H cm); 35068-136, gift of Dr. James B. Richardson III

Bag: Commercial wool and cotton, cardboard, glass, paper, brass; H 4.3 in. (5.3 L x 14.5 W x 11.0 H cm); 35068-131, gift of Dr. James B. Richardson III

Needle case: Commercial silk and cotton, unidentified stuffing, glass, cardboard, paper, ink, unidentified shell; W 4.8 in. (7.0 L x 12.5 W x 3.3 H cm); 35068-134, gift of Dr. James B. Richardson III

Boot pincushion: Commercial wool and cotton, unidentified stuffing, glass, paper, commercial silk; L 4.4 in. (11.5 L x 7.6 W x 2.5 H cm); 35068-100, gift of Dr. James B. Richardson III

FAN

Maliseet?, 1850-1860

Woodlands women made birch bark fan handles, embroidered delicately with porcupine quills. Euro-American merchandisers then added the fans made of feathers and stuffed birds.

Paper birch bark (*Betula papyrifera*), Eastern Meadow Lark (*Sturnella magna*), unidentified down feathers, porcupine quills (*Erethizon dorsatum*), commercial dye, commercial cotton, glass; L 14.5 in. (37.2 L x 23.5 W x 5.0 H cm); 35068-2, gift of Dr. James B. Richardson III

THREE BAGS

Iroquois, 1850-1875

Iroquois bags and purses in innumerable variations on the same theme sold in the greatest numbers. Their makers incorporated an assortment of materials—beads, rickrack, ribbon—to make the bags eyecatching to both tourists and Native people, who also used them.

(Left to right) Commercial cotton, glass, paper, brass, commercial silk, silver; L 7.5 in. (19.5 L x 18.0 W cm); 35068-17, gift of Dr. James B. Richardson III

Commercial silk and cotton, glass, paper, silver; L 7.1 in. (18.5 L x 18.5 W cm); 35068-35, gift of Dr. James B. Richardson III

Commercial cotton, glass, paper, commercial silk, silver; L 8.2 in. (21.0 L x 16.0 W cm); 35068-36, gift of Dr. James B. Richardson III

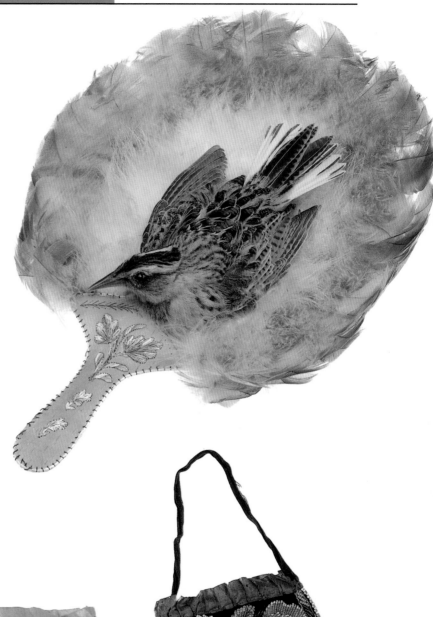

MAKING BEADED WHIMSIES, 1978. Just like the maternal generations before her, Sarah Dubuc (Yeh Sah Ges), Turtle clan, Tuscarora, carries on her family's artistic traditions.

(Photographer unknown. Iroquois Indian Museum, IIM 74.22A-24A)

PICTURE FRAME

Ann Printup (1958-), Sanborn, New York, Bear clan, Cayuga/Tuscarora, 1992

WALL WATCH POCKET

Ann Printup (1958-), Sanborn, New York, Bear clan, Cayuga/Tuscarora, 1992

Iroquois women continue to make Victorian-style beaded whimsies, as well as beaded clan medallions and other items, for both Iroquois use and sale to non-Indians.

Picture frame: Commercial cotton, cardboard, glass, plastic, paper; L 9.8 in. (25.1 L x 24.8 W cm); 35418-2

Watch pocket: Commercial cotton, glass, plastic, paper, polyester; L 10.7 in. (27.5 L x 9.2 W x 5.8 H cm); 35418-1

SEWING BASKET

Penobscot?, 1880-1900

SEWING SET

Abenaki?, ca. 1910

Everyone made baskets. I was probably six or seven when I made my first ash basket. Almost every man, woman, and child on the island knew how to make them. We'd gather together in our homes every day to work. It was how we survived. It was how we kept a connection to the past.

LAWRENCE SHAY, PENOBSCOT, 1995 [17]

Women created the elaborate fancy baskets that appealed to Victorian tastes, while men prepared the splints and made the utilitarian workbaskets. During the winter families made the baskets, and when summer came, they packed their belongings and moved to resorts to sell their arts. In 1890 the United States Bureau of the Census reported Iroquois basketmakers on the St. Regis (Akwesasne), Oneida, Cattaraugus, and Onondaga Reservations. During that same year Mohawk families at St. Regis netted an average of $250, nearly ten times as much as they made from crop sales. In Maine 66 percent of the Penobscot population listed basketmaking as their major source of income by 1900.

Basket: Black ash (*Fraxinus nigra*), commercial dye, sweetgrass (*Hierochloe odorata*); L 12.3 in. (31.5 L x 27.0 W x 11.5 H cm); 34937-1, gift of Miriam D. Richardson

Sewing set: Black ash (*Fraxinus nigra*), commercial silk and cotton, sweetgrass (*Hierochloe odorata*), unidentified bone; L 8.8 in. (22.8 L x 15.2 W x 2.5 H cm); 34937-46 a-d, gift of Miriam D. Richardson

MOOSE HAIR GLASSES CASE
Huron? or Micmac?, 1850-1860

SPECTACLES
Northeastern United States, early 1800s

Using hair from the mane of a moose to create delicate embroidered patterns is a remarkable application of Nature's materials.

The history of its development is equally fascinating. Woodlands people taught the Ursuline nuns who arrived in French Canada in the seventeenth century how to work in moose hair and birch bark. When the religious order established mission schools, the nuns trained Huron women to do fine embroidery in European floral designs, using the moose hair.

Case: Commercial wool, paper, commercial silk, moose hair (*Alces alces*), dye; L 6.2 in. (15.8 L x 4.2 W cm); 35460-1. Spectacles: brass, glass, gold?; W 4.3 in. (11.0 W x 2.5 H cm); 16049-4, gift of Mrs. Davenport Hooker

MOCCASINS
Iroquois, 1850-1875

Iroquois women continued to make traditional objects, such as these moccasins, to wear on dress occasions. Moccasins were also popular with non-Native clientele, who considered them both exotic and unmistakably "native" and yet could wear them at home as house slippers.

Tanned hide, commercial cotton and silk, glass, paper, silver; L 9.0 in. (23.0 L x 9.5 W x 7.0 H cm); 35068-66 a & b, gift of Dr. James B. Richardson III

MOOSE HAIR TRAY
Huron? or Micmac?, ca. 1850s

Paper birch bark (*Betula papyrifera*), moose hair (*Alces alces*), porcupine quills (*Erethizon dorsatum*), dye, commercial cotton; D 7.1 in. (4.2 H x 18.5 D cm); 33346-14, gift of Dr. James B. Richardson III

QUILLED CHAIR
Micmac, 1870-1900

The Iroquois were not the only Woodlands nations to make objects for the flourishing tourist trade. The Abenaki, Huron, Maliseet, Micmac, Passamaquoddy, and Penobscot, among others, also participated in this economy.

Some Native groups specialized in particular techniques and crafts. Eastern Canada's Micmac people rechanneled their traditional quillworking skills into producing quilled patterns on birch bark for Victorian customers. Objects ranged from small lidded boxes to chair seats and backs totally appliquéd in quills.

Pine? (*Pinus* sp.), birch bark (*Betula papyrifera*), dye, porcupine quills (*Erethizon dorsatum*), spruce root?, sweetgrass (*Hierochloe odorata*), glue, sealing wax?; H 35.4 in. (41.5 L x 50.0 W x 90.2 H cm); 35734-1 a-c, gift of Dr. James B. Richardson III

AGNES (LEFT) AND CHARLOTTE SUNDOWN (RIGHT) POSE WITH THEIR BASKETS AT TONAWANDA RESERVATION, CA. 1910.

(Photographer unknown. Rochester Museum and Science Center, Rochester, New York, 1938)

GENERATIONS OF IRONWORKERS

Ironwork provides the Indians with an honorable way to make a living. Young ironworkers carry the reputation of their fathers, or uncles, to each job, but you earn your own name among the men, and a new reputation is born for your sons to live up to.

RON LaFRANCE, MOHAWK, 1987[18]

Walking the STEEL

SMITH SURE DOES MAKE THE CONNECTIONS

YEAH! THE GUY IS REALLY GOIN' PLACES

CRUNCH

STAYING SAFE, 1970s. All Pittsburgh ironworkers received a safety manual with cartoons illustrating dangerous situations. These cartoons were meant to help relieve the tension of the stressful job while illustrating a point of safety.

(American Bridge Safety Manual, page 19, 35825-2)

Iroquois ironworkers, especially the Mohawks, are legendary for their dizzying work in erecting skyscrapers and steel bridges. Mohawks have walked the steel and worked on nearly all of New York's towering buildings, including the Empire State Building, the Chrysler Building, and Rockefeller Center. Many came to Pittsburgh to work on the U.S. Steel Building, the Civic Arena, and the Fort Pitt Bridge, among others.

Generations of Iroquois men have followed in this profession, which began in 1886 with the construction of the Canadian Pacific Railway Bridge across the Saint Lawrence River. To obtain permission to build the southern abutment of the bridge on reservation land, the construction company agreed to hire men from the Kahnawake Reservation. *Putting riveting tools in the Mohawks' hands was like putting ham with eggs. They were natural-born bridgemen,* said one construction company official.[19]

Some Iroquois compare working the iron to an earlier chapter in their history. Once as hunters and warriors they left their homes for extended periods to travel long distances, earning a living for their families back home, making their personal reputations, and seeking adventure.

I see ironwork as the last employment [of the warrior]. We travel [to the cities] in gangs like a hunting party, and the building is the hunt. To climb a column, stand on top of it, and feel the wind is like climbing a mountain.

RON LaFRANCE, MOHAWK, 1994[20]

Before mandatory safety regulations, ironworkers faced perilous risks of falling. *Every family on my reservation [Akwesasne] has lost at least one member to a fall,* says Ron LaFrance, who himself once fell three stories.[21] Even today Iroquois ironworkers prefer to work without safety lines, stating that these inhibit free movement.

Today Native people from all over the country learn how to be ironworkers in the National Ironworkers Training Program for American Indians. Walking the high steel earns a good wage, and it is also a source of pride.

TOOL BELT
Mine Safety Appliance Company, 1980

HARD HAT
Northeastern United States, 1975

SAFETY MANUAL
Northeastern United States, 1970s

An ironworker carries in his tool belt two spud wrenches, symbols of his job. The pointed handle on each wrench is used to align the holes of two pieces of steel before the beams are bolted together with the other end.

Pittsburgh's American Bridge, which employed Iroquois ironworkers to help erect the city's bridges, provided all workers with a safety manual of rules.

Tool belt: Commercial cotton, nylon, brass, commercial leather, steel, copper; W 46.8 in. (54.5 L x 119.0 W x 14.0 H cm); 35825-3 a-e, gift of American Bridge

Hard hat: Fiberglass, paint, plastic, polyester?, rubber, rayon?, steel, paper, ink, adhesive; L 11.8 in. (30.2 L x 26.8 W x 14.5 H cm); 35825-1, gift of American Bridge

Manual: Ink, paper, steel; L 7.0 in. (18.2 L x 10.5 W cm); 35825-2, gift of American Bridge

T-SHIRT
Harold (Jack) Johnson, Ohsweken, Ontario, Mohawk, 1992

This T-shirt compares the Native ironworker, renowned for his fearless daring at great heights, with the profile of an eagle, the proud bird that also soars aloft.

Commercial cotton, polyester, ink; W 31.2 in. (74.0 L x 79.5 W cm); 35732-2

NORTH | SOUTH | EAST | WEST

The Lakota and Their Neighbors on the Great Plains

WE INDIANS THINK OF THE EARTH AND THE WHOLE UNIVERSE
AS A NEVER-ENDING CIRCLE, AND IN THIS CIRCLE, MAN IS JUST
ANOTHER ANIMAL. THE BUFFALO AND THE COYOTE ARE OUR
BROTHERS; THE BIRDS, OUR COUSINS. WE END OUR PRAYERS
WITH THE WORDS "ALL MY RELATIONS"—AND THAT INCLUDES
EVERYTHING THAT GROWS, CRAWLS, RUNS, CREEPS, HOPS, AND
FLIES.

JENNY LEADING CLOUD, LAKOTA 1992[1]

A people without history is like the wind on the buffalo grass.

A PLACE IN TIME

The Lakota (Western Sioux) live on five reservations in South and North Dakota in a region of geographic diversity and climatic fluctuation.[3] Mixed grasses cover rolling hills interrupted by sandhills, badlands, buttes, and canyons formed by the Missouri River and its tributaries.

These people have not lived in this region long. With the acquisition of European-introduced horses and guns in quantity, the Lakota and their equestrian neighbors entered the Plains, abandoning their woodland homes and gardens in pursuit of the vast herds of American bison and other game animals. According to the winter count kept by American Horse, the first group of Oglala Lakota arrived at the Black Hills in 1775.[4] They roamed throughout the region for some one hundred years before being settled on reservations.

It was not the first time they had traveled to the Plains, but it was the first time they stayed. There the seasonally nomadic Lakota shared the environment with long-term residents who lived in permanent village settlements along the rivers and practiced agriculture. Nature offered not one, but various ways for humans to live on the Plains.

The GREAT PLAINS

TOM HAUKAAS, CREATOR OF THE CARNEGIE WINTER COUNT, AT HOME, ABOUT 1995. *My winter count is an individual interpretation of factors affecting the history of the Heyata Wičasa, the Sicangu Lakota people of the Rosebud Reservation and many other places. It is from a contemporary viewpoint. It purposefully includes community and national events, men and women, full-bloods and mixed-bloods, as an attempt to capture the richness and complexity of our tribe.*

(Photo by Harold L. Haukaas)

THE CARNEGIE WINTER COUNT, 1995

Groups of people record their history even when they do not have written languages. They do so by passing down events orally or by recording them pictorially. The Lakota created winter counts, which are drawings of historical events recorded on animal hides or muslin.

In the past, every Lakota band had a keeper of the winter count. Once a year the leaders reviewed the important events of the previous year and together selected the single most significant one, which the keeper added to the long list of annual pictographs, consisting of as many as 200 entries. He could recite the story of each successive winter on this lengthy winter count, thereby passing on history orally. Such memorable events as smallpox epidemics, wars, school attendance, and the move from tipi to cabin were noted on the winter counts. Tribal members could recall the year of their birth by the event associated with their birth date.

CARNEGIE WINTER COUNT

Thomas Red Owl Haukaas, M.D.
(1950-), Sicaṅġu (Brulé)
Lakota/Creole, 1995

In this unique contemporary winter count, Dr. Haukaas depicted 125 yearly events, from 1868-1869 to 1992-1993, for the Sicaṅġu Lakota people on the Rosebud Reservation in South Dakota. In place of the count keeper, he created a drawing book that gives an explanation for each year.

Dr. Haukaas began the winter count with the creation of the reservation in 1868-1869 and ended with the 500th anniversary of Columbus's encounter with Native Americans.

*1977-1978: Dirt Bags Winter
The Supreme Court's ruling in
ROSEBUD V. KNEIP reduced the legal
boundaries of the Rosebud
[Reservation]. The sense of loss was
keenly felt. An elder and his grandson
were dressing to dance. The grandfather
took a paint bag filled with red earth
and daubed his own face. Then he took
the one with yellow earth paint and
decorated his grandson's face. The boy
asked: "Grandfather, what does the
Supreme Court ruling mean to our
people?" Grandfather pointed his lips
toward the paint bags and said: "If we
don't watch it, these will be all that's
left of the Rosebud."*

*1992-1993: Communication Winter
The Columbian Quincentenary was
not a time of celebration on the
Rosebud. Governor George Mickelson
declared it the Year of Reconciliation in
an effort to open real dialogue between
Indians and non-Indians in the state of
South Dakota.*

Brain-tanned deer hide (*Odocoileus* sp.),
ink, commercial paint, nylon sinew; L
48.4 in. (123.0 L x 95.7 W cm);
36025-1a

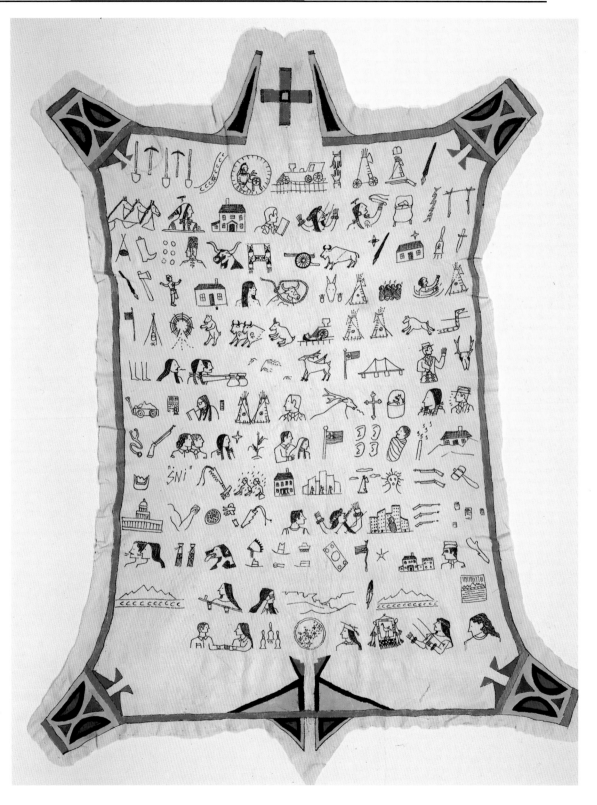

The keeper of the winter count was a good man. . . . This man possessed a skill which he used for the benefit of the whole tribe. He kept a history of the people for their remembrance as far back as history could record it. Thus the people would have a good understanding of their origins and early history and understand how they arrived at the place where they were in the present.

BEN BLACK BEAR, JR., LAKOTA, 1976[5]

By the 1930s the tradition of the winter count had generally ceased. Thomas Red Owl Haukaas has created the Carnegie Winter Count from a 1990s viewpoint, including social and political issues that have affected the lives of Lakota people up to the present.

THE UNIVERSE

The sun, the moon, the morning star, the evening star, the north star, the seven stars, the six stars, the rainbow—these are all WAKAN *[sacred].*

GOOD SEAT, LAKOTA, CA. 1900[6]

On the Plains the landscape is vast and the sky looms large. Plains people have looked to the geographic features of the Earth and to the stars in the sky above for finding the way and making decisions.

All humans would be directionless on Earth without celestial aid from the observable sky, without the sun and the other stars to help us locate ourselves in space and time. The Plains tribes practiced naked-eye astronomy and observation. The Lakota used the stars to guide them in finding their way and to time their hunting, gathering, and ritual activities. Philosophically they believed that the geography of the Earth is a reflection of the star world.

SHIELD WITH COVER
Crow, collected 1904

A Plains man treasured his shield, which protected him both physically and spiritually in battle. When a warrior dreamed of an image such as this one, a man inside the sun, he painted it on the cover of his shield.

Shield: buffalo rawhide (*Bison bison*); cover: tanned deer hide (*Odocoileus* sp.), paint, clay, sinew; D 20.9 in. (3.0 H x 53.0 D cm); 2418-116a

Traveling by night they go by the big dipper. Handle is in the west in the evening and when they are going out they figure so much from the handle toward the south and they allow so much space.

BLACK ELK, LAKOTA, 1931[7]

The stars and planets of most significance to Plains people are Venus (Morning or Evening Star), Ursa Major (Big Dipper), and the Pleiades. Each tribe has its own name for the various constellations. The Arapaho call Ursa Major the Broken Backbone. In a folktale the Lakota tell how the Seven Little Girls, or Pleiades, were placed in the sky.

Venus shines brighter than any other planet or star in the sky, and the Lakota people have incorporated it as a symbol into their myth and ceremony. The Morning Star dominates Lakota quilt design. Lakota women began making quilts as an alternative to buffalo robes in the late nineteenth century, when bison were no longer available. Quilters learned the technique from Euro-American women in government schools and church guilds, and most likely singled out the Star of Bethlehem pattern as a favorite because of its resemblance to their traditional Morning Star design.

Plains artists pay homage to the centrality, power, and importance of the sun and the sky with depictions on ceremonial and personal-power objects. The major annual ceremony of renewal is dedicated to the sun.

CAMP WITH SHIELD ON TRIPOD, ABOUT 1880.
In the early morning a wife would place her husband's shield on a tripod outside their tipi. Throughout the day she rotated the shield to follow the daily movements of the sun. The shield absorbed the sun's powerful rays and protected the family group in the tipi.
(Photo by Harrison J. Thornton. W. H. Over Museum, 43.01)

If one wishes for the best of visions, he must seek it of the Sun. He must gaze at the Sun until he sees the vision. . . . All the Sun Dancers sound a large whistle while dancing and look at the Sun as it moves. . . .

If they wish for many buffalo, they will sing of them; if victory, sing of it; and if they wish to bring good weather, they will sing of it.

THOMAS TYON, LAKOTA, 1911-1912[8]

Plains people address the four cardinal directions plus two more, the zenith above and the nadir below, during every ceremonial undertaking. *Good things come by four,* says Joe Medicine Crow of the Crow nation.[9] Four is an important number to Plains people. It is the number that occurs most frequently in nature—four seasons, four winds, four directions.

In former times the Lakota grouped all their activities by four's. This was because they recognized four directions: the west, the north, the east, and the south; four divisions of time: the day, the night, the moon, and the year; four parts to everything that grows from the ground: the roots, the stem, the leaves, and the fruit; four kinds of things that breathe: those that crawl, those that fly, those that walk on four legs, and those that walk on two legs; four things above the world: the sun, the moon, the sky, and the stars; . . . four periods of human life: babyhood, childhood, adulthood, and old age; and, finally, mankind had four fingers on each hand, four toes on each foot, and the thumbs and the great toes of each taken together are four. Since the Great Spirit caused everything to be in four's, mankind should do everything possible in four's.

THOMAS TYON, LAKOTA,
CA. 1911-1912[10]

Look toward the West!
Your Grandfather
is sitting there looking this way.
Pray to Him! Pray to Him!
He is sitting there looking this way.

Look toward the North!
Your Grandfather
is sitting there looking this way.
Pray to Him! Pray to Him!
He is sitting there looking this way.

Look toward the East!
Your Grandfather
is sitting there looking this way.
Pray to Him! Pray to Him!
He is sitting there looking this way.

Look toward the South!
Your Grandfather
is sitting there looking this way.
Pray to Him! Pray to Him!
He is sitting there looking this way.

Look up above!
The Great Spirit,
He is sitting above us.
Pray to Him! Pray to Him!
He is sitting there looking this way.

Look down to the Earth!
Your Grandmother
is lying beneath you.
Pray to Her! Pray to Her!
She is lying there, listening to your prayers.

LAKOTA SONG

RATTLES
Arapaho, collected 1903

These doughnut-shaped rattles represent both the sun and the moon. Arapaho boys and men belonged to a series of age-related societies throughout their lives. Young men who advanced to the Star Company, the second level of the societies, used this type of rattle.

Left: Rawhide, tanned hide, Black-billed Magpie feathers (*Pica pica*), male Sage Grouse under-tail covert feathers (*Centrocercus urophasianus*), Golden Eagle feather (*Aquila chrysaetos*), unidentified wood, pebbles, paint, sinew; L 23.6 in. (60.0 L x 13.0 W x 3.5 H cm); 3179-201. Right: Rawhide, tanned hide, Sage Grouse under-tail covert feathers (*Centrocercus urophasianus*), Great Horned Owl body and wing feathers (*Bubo virginianus*), pebbles, unidentified wood, sinew, paint, commercial dye; L 22.8 in. (58.0 L x 9.5 W x 3.0 H cm); 3179-287

ROBE
Arapaho, collected 1903

The Arapaho call Ursa Major (the Big Dipper) the Broken Backbone. About the painting on this robe, collector Cleaver Warden, an Arapaho, notes: *Designs surrounding this broken backbone are shapes, colors of mountains, hills, rivers, ravines, valleys, creeks, two bears' claws.*[11]

Cow hide (*Bos taurus*), paint, clay; W 42.1 in. (102.0 L x 107.0 W cm); 3179-294

PARFLECHE
Arapaho, collected 1903

Plains women were often inspired by the environment around them when creating their geometric paintings. Only each individual artist knew the meaning of her design. An Arapaho woman thought about her world and painted an abstract landscape on this folded, rawhide container, called a parfleche. This is what she said about her painting:

Six rows of colored designs reproduce the whole appearance of the earth (rough). Two white lines traversing two center designs denote the paths of the sun and moon. White and blue lines at the edge of the parfleche mean the "ocean" and horizon. Blue paint, the sky; red paint, the earth; green paint, the grass; white field, water. This parfleche denotes the winter season.[12]

Cow rawhide (*Bos taurus*), commercial paint; L 24.6 in. (62.5 L x 38.5 W x 6.5 H cm); 3179-308

THE CIRCLE

The Oglala [Lakota] believe the circle to be sacred because the Great Spirit caused everything in nature to be round. . . . The sun and the sky, the earth and the moon are round like a shield. . . . Everything that grows from the ground is round like the stem of a tree. . . . The day, the night, and the moon go in a circle above the sky. Therefore the circle is a symbol of these divisions of time and hence the symbol of all time.

For these reasons the Oglala make their tipis circular, their camp circle circular, and sit in a circle in all ceremonies.

THOMAS TYON, LAKOTA, CA. 1910[13]

NELLIE STAR BOY MENARD, QUILTMAKER, AND HER GRANDDAUGHTER, TERESA STAR CHIEF, DISPLAY MRS. MENARD'S STAR QUILT, 1994.

(Photo by Marsha C. Bol. Carnegie Museum of Natural History)

STAR QUILT

Nellie Star Boy Menard (1910-), Sicaṅgu (Brulé) Lakota, Rosebud Reservation, South Dakota, 1994

Nellie Star Boy Menard learned to make Lakota star quilts because she needed them for the memorial service of her son's death. Her mother showed her how to make the star and sew the pieces together. Since then she has made dozens to honor relatives and to use as gifts for community giveaways.

At home Mrs. Menard is revered as an elder authority on the traditional arts by her own Rosebud community. Beyond the reservation she received in 1995 an NEA National Heritage Fellowship—this country's highest honor—for her lifetime achievement as a master folk artist.

Commercial cotton, polyester fill; L 93.5 in. (237.5 L x 199.5 W cm); 35882-1

ZUNI HUNTING CHARMS
Dinah Gaspar, Zuni, New Mexico, 1991

In their work, Native artists make reference to stars and constellations, as well as to orientation and directionality in the cosmos. This set of Zuni hunting charms, popularly called fetishes, depicts the animal guardians of the six directions.

Clockwise from upper left: Bear (West): Calcite or dolomite, paint; Badger (South): Calcite or onyx, paint; Eagle (Above): Marble, paint; Mountain lion (North): Serpentine, paint; Mole (Below): Jet; Wolf (East): Marble, paint; avg. L 2.6 in. (avg. 6.5 L x 2.2 W x 2.8 H cm); 35154-3 a-f

Sky Watching

Most Native American tribes observe the sky, incorporating the movements of the celestial bodies into their own lives. By watching the stars change position, disappear, and reappear throughout the seasons, Native people determine when to plant and harvest, when to hunt and gather, and when to carry out religious activities.

ARIZONA AND NEW MEXICO

HOPI STAR KATSINA
SOHU TIHU
Hopi, Arizona, ca. 1904

Cottonwood (*Populus* sp.), paint, unidentified feather, female American Kestrel feather (*Falco sparverius*), commercial cotton, commercial dye; H 12.3 in. (15.0 W x 31.5 H cm); 3165-96

NAVAJO SAND PAINTING: FATHER SKY AND MOTHER EARTH
Juanita Stevens, Navajo, Arizona, early 1900s

Particle board, pine (*Pinus* sp.), oak (*Quercus* sp.), sandstone, glue, steel, copper, acrylic; W 24.8 in. (63.5 W x 63.5 H cm); 35943-1

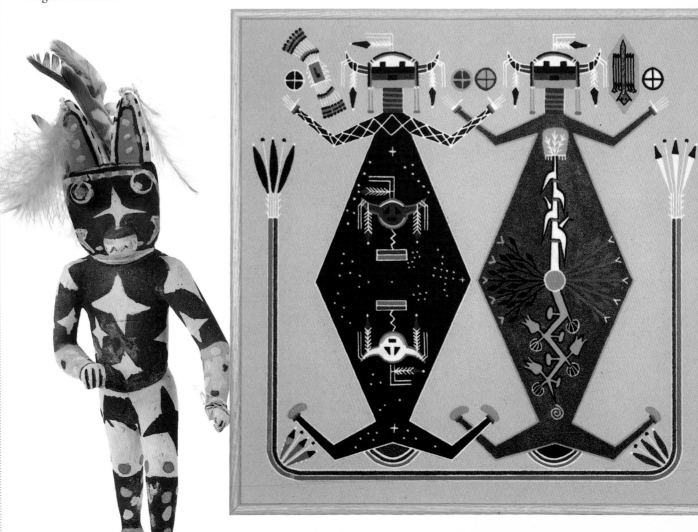

As Indian people have developed and evolved throughout the ages, we have done so alongside all of these other creatures—buffalo, prairie dogs, eagles—all these different things that we learned from. FRED DuBRAY, LAKOTA, 1994[15]

HEADDRESS AND TRAILER

Lakota, collected 1888

Lakota elders told Dr. James R. Walker in 1912: *Only those who have accomplished much are entitled to wear the buffalo horns.*[14] Sitting Bull, the renowned Lakota leader, may have owned this headdress.

Immature Golden Eagle feathers (*Aquila chrysaetos*), buffalo horns (*Bison bison*), buffalo hide (*Bison bison*), Rough-legged Hawk primary feathers (*Buteo lagopus*), commercial cotton canvas and thread, commercial wool stroud, tanned hide, tinned metal, adhesive, sinew; L 80.7 in. (205.0 L x 42.0 W cm); 23102-16843 a & b, gift of John A. Beck

ALL My Relatives

ESPECIALLY BUFFALO

Lakota philosophy considers the world as a unified whole in which everything is interrelated. Animals are considered to be relatives that share the Earth as partners with humans. For this reason ceremonies close with the words *all my relatives.* The most important of these relatives continues to be the American bison, popularly known as the buffalo, with whom Plains people have maintained a special relationship. Ernie Robinson, a member of the InterTribal Bison Cooperative, an organization dedicated to restoring buffalo herds on the reservations, says: *The story of the buffalo is also the story of the tribe. . . . They were almost extinct, but now they're coming back strong. They're survivors . . . just like us.*[16]

Throughout their history Plains people have been intimately linked with the buffalo and other large game animals. The Lakota changed their living habits after they acquired a sufficient number of horses to permit the men to hunt more advantageously. They moved permanently onto the Plains from the woodlands of Minnesota, following the roaming buffalo herds from place to place across the great

ROBE

Dorothy Little Elk (1957-),
Sicaṅǧu (Brulé) Lakota,
Rosebud Reservation, South
Dakota, 1992-1993

It took Dorothy Little Elk
six months to make this
beaded robe from an aborted
buffalo fetus. She says,
however, *My baby slowed
down my progress.*[22]

Buffalo fetus hide (*Bison biso*n),
glass, steel, brass, rawhide,
porcupine quills (*Erethizon
dorsatum*), nylon sinew,
commercial dye; W 35.8 in.
(76.0 L x 91.0 W cm); 35588-1

**AT A CHEYENNE SUMMER
CAMP, STRIPS OF BEEF HANG
ON RACKS TO DRY IN THE
SUN, 1895.** Plains women
continued to use the same
techniques to process beef
received as annuity payments
as they had used to preserve
the buffalo before it became
extinct.

(Photographer unknown. Smithsonian
Institution, 43, 118-A)

**BISON BULL IN ITS NATURAL
HABITAT.**

(Photo by Harvey Payne)

THE INTERTRIBAL BISON COOPERATIVE

*Buffalo can bring our people
together. Now it's our turn to
take care of them.*

FRED DuBRAY,
PRESIDENT OF THE
INTERTRIBAL BISON
COOPERATIVE[23]

Founded in 1990, the
cooperative is head-
quartered in Rapid City,
South Dakota. In 1996 thirty-
six tribes belonged to the coop
and oversaw some 7,000
buffalo in the various tribal
herds. The cooperative actively
reestablishes buffalo herds on
Indian lands in ways that
promote not only economic
development but cultural and
spiritual revitalization as well.
As DuBray points out, *We
recognize the buffalo as a symbol
of our strength and unity; . . . as
we bring our herds back to
health we will also bring our
people back to health.*[24]

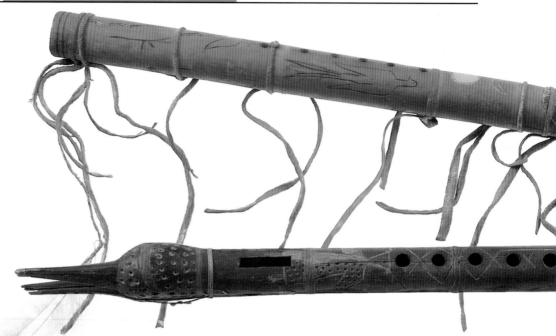

ELK: THE IRRESISTIBLE ONE

The Elk declared . . . all the women are crazy about me.

JOSEPH WHITE BULL, LAKOTA, 1932[25]

In addition to being good to eat, certain large game animals, such as elk and deer, figure significantly in the beliefs of Plains Indians. The Lakota, for example, associate the bull elk with the power to attract females. Observing his behavior in nature, the people noted the male elk's amorous activities that successfully lured female elk to him.

Since the Lakota believe that the powers of animals are available to humans, certain men in the past became associated with elk through dreams and received supernatural abilities to attract women. Understandably, the elk was a favorite animal among young men.

Far to the west,
Far by the sky
Stands a blue Elk.
That Elk standing yonder
Watches o'er all the females
On the earth.

Far to the east,
Far by the sky
Stands a blue Elk.
That Elk standing yonder
Watches o'er all the females
On the earth.

FLAT IRON, LAKOTA, CA. 1900[26]

BEN REIFEL PLAYS THE COURTING FLUTE, ROSEBUD RESERVATION, SOUTH DAKOTA, CA. 1925.

(Photo by John A. Anderson. Nebraska State Historical Society, A547:1-88)

The Circle of RELATIVES

WOMEN: THE ARTS OF MOTHERS, SISTERS, AND WIVES

My dear sisters, the women. . . . By your hands the family moves. You have been given the knowledge of making clothing and of feeding the family.

WHITE BUFFALO CALF WOMAN[33]

It is a woman, the mythical White Buffalo Calf Woman, who is the heroine of the Lakota culture. She brought the sacred pipe to the people.

Lakota women were partners with men in the work of supporting a family, although they had separate spheres of activity. One way Lakota women cared for their families was to make and decorate beautiful clothing for all members, including their brothers to whom they had a lifelong obligation. Fine apparel for their families was and still is a sign of affection and honor from wives, mothers, sisters, and grandmothers.

Lakota women, respected for their skill as artists, excelled in quillwork and beadwork. Artists ingeniously converted porcupine quills, readily found in nature, into elaborate surface decorations. When glass beads were imported from Europe as a trade item in the nineteenth century, Plains women stitched them into their own traditional patterns, so that today beadwork is regarded as a purely indigenous art form. Lakota women have maintained an unbroken tradition of making quill- and beadwork embroidery, continuing to do beautiful work today.

The Lakota call a woman who creates wonderful things with her hands NAPE WAŚTE *or "good hands."*

ROSALIE LITTLE THUNDER, LAKOTA, 1995[34]

MAN'S MOCCASINS
Lakota, collected 1900-1914

Women sometimes expressed affection for men and children by beading every surface of their moccasins, even the soles. These moccasins were worn for special events such as weddings, honoring ceremonies, and burials.

Tanned hide, glass, commercial cotton, sinew, tinned metal, unidentified feather, commercial dye; L 11.0 in. (28.0 L x 11.0 W x 9.5 H cm); 23102-16895 a & b, gift of John A. Beck

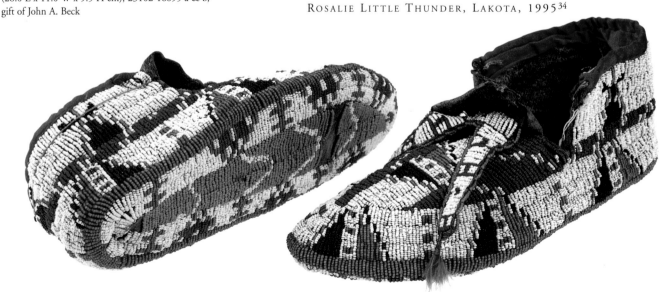

**LAKOTA MOTHER WITH HER THREE CHILDREN
CLOTHED IN ELABORATELY BEADED OUTFITS,
ROSEBUD RESERVATION, SOUTH DAKOTA, 1895-1899.**

(Photo by Jesse H. Bratley. Photo Archives, Denver Museum of Natural
History, BR61-309)

PIPE BAG

Lakota, collected ca. 1899

Pipe bags were used by Plains men but made by
women. Both regarded the pouch as a work of art.

Tanned hide, glass, sinew, tinned metal, horsehair (*Equus
caballus*), porcupine quill (*Erethizon dorsatum*), commercial
dye; L 35.1 in. (89.2 L x 20.4 W cm); 1171-26

A FAMILY OF ARTISTS AND THEIR WORK

Rosalie Little Thunder (Lakota) was born on the Rosebud Reservation and now lives in Rapid City, South Dakota, with her five children and five grandchildren. She makes her living doing fine traditional beadwork and consistently wins prizes at regional and national art fairs.

All her children, from her adult daughter Deborah to her youngest Becky, do beadwork. They learned from their mother, who not only teaches her children but also provides a stimulating atmosphere. A table, ladened with containers of beads, sinew, and pieces of tanned hide, sits in the corner of the living room near the television. Books and exhibition catalogues filled with historic beadwork photographs are placed strategically around the house, including in the bathroom, as well as in the car. Photographs of museum pieces hang in frames on the wall, as do prize ribbons that family members have won. Most importantly, the children see their mother doing beadwork, and they often contribute to the pieces, resulting in collaborative works.

Rosalie tells her children, *Anybody can be a secretary, but you can make a living as a beadworker.*[35] As artists they are able to work at home and raise their children surrounded by their extended family, in much the same way as the traditional tipi community of the past.

AMULET
Rebecca Good Bear (1985-), Sicaṅgu (Brulé) / Sans Arc / Minneconjou Lakota, 1992

BELT BUCKLE
Leonard Good Bear (1947-), Sans Arc / Minneconjou Lakota, 1995

BAG
Barbara Kills-in-Water-Hernandez (1969-), Sicaṅgu (Brulé) Lakota, 1993

PIPE BAG
Deborah Little Thunder (1967-), Sicaṅgu (Brulé) Lakota, 1993

Amulet: Polyester fill, tanned deer hide (*Odocoileus* sp), glass, nylon sinew; L 4.9 in. (12.5 L x 5.5 W cm); 35415-11. Buckle: Commercial leather, steel, glass, polyester, porcupine quill (*Erethizon dorsatum*), nylon sinew; W 4.1 in. (8.2 L x 10.5 W cm); 36076-3. Bag: Tanned deer hide (*Odocoileus* sp.), glass, tinned metal, horsehair (*Equus caballus*), steel, nylon sinew; L 9.7 in. (24.5 L x 24.0 W cm); 35588-2. Pipe bag: Tanned deer hide (*Odocoileus* sp.), glass, tinned metal, horsehair (*Equus caballus*), brass, steel, nylon sinew; L 37.8 in. (96.0 L x 22.0 W cm); 35883-1

ROSALIE LITTLE THUNDER AND HER FAMILY, 1996.
Front row (left to right): Deborah Little Thunder, Rosalie
Little Thunder, and Jon Good Bear. Back row (left to right):
Barbara Kills-in-Water-Hernandez, Amy Good Bear, Rebecca
Good Bear.

(Photo by Amy Good Bear)

KNIFE SHEATH
Jon Good Bear (1982-), Sicangu (Brulé) /
Sans Arc / Minneconjou Lakota, 1996

Tanned deer hide (*Odocoileus* sp.), glass, tinned
metal, brass, nylon sinew; L 17.2 in. (44.0 L x
20.0 W cm); 36209-4

PIPE BAG
Barbara Kills-in-Water-Hernandez (1969-),
Sicangu (Brulé) Lakota, 1996

Tanned deer hide (*Odocoileus* sp.), glass, horsehair
(*Equus caballus*), tinned metal, bone, brass, nylon
sinew; L 33.7 in. (86.5 L x 22.0 W cm); 36209-3

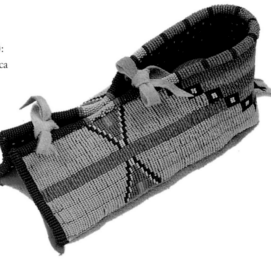

DOLL CRADLE
Amy Good Bear (1978-), Sicangu
(Brulé) / Sans Arc / Minneconjou Lakota,
1996

Tanned hide, glass, commercial cotton, nylon
sinew, commercial wool; L 10.2 in. (26.0 L x
12.0 W x 8.4 H cm); 36294-3

MOCCASINS AND LEGGINGS
Rosalie Little Thunder (1949-), Sicangu
(Brulé) Lakota, 1996

Moccasins: Tanned hide, glass, tinned metal,
horsehair (*Equus caballus*), commercial cotton,
nylon sinew; L 9.9 in. (25.6 L x 10.5 W x 9.9
H cm); 36294-1 a & b. Leggings: Tanned hide,
glass, nylon sinew, nickel silver, ochre?; L 16.9
in. (43.0 L x 27.0 W cm); 36294-2 a & b

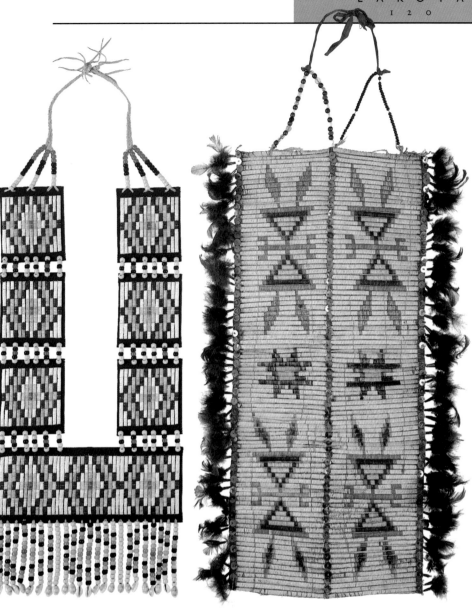

WOMAN'S BREASTPLATE (LEFT)

Cathy and Victor Young, Oglala and Sicaṅgu (Brulé)
Lakota, Rosebud Reservation, South Dakota, 1994

MAN'S BREASTPLATE (RIGHT)

Lakota, early 1900s

Breastplates constructed of wrapped porcupine quills were worn as adornment by both women and men. Victor Young and his wife Cathy, a member of the New Holy family of quillworkers from Pine Ridge Reservation, South Dakota, continue the artistic tradition of quillwork.

Woman's breastplate: Porcupine quill (*Erethizon dorsatum*), rawhide, commercial cotton, tanned hide, glass, cowry shell (*Cypraea* sp.), nylon sinew, commercial dye; L 35.4 in. (90.0 L x 29.3 W cm); 35716-1

Man's breastplate: Commercial cotton, porcupine quill (*Erethizon dorsatum*), rawhide, tinned metal, unidentified feather, glass, plastic, unidentified wood, sinew, commercial dye, paint; L 39.4 in. (100.0 L x 43.5 W cm); 35752-122, gift of Benjamin D. Bernstein in memory of Evelyn Glauser Bernstein

FEMALE AND MALE DOLLS

Sandra Brewer (1964-), Lakota, Cheyenne River Reservation,
South Dakota, 1992

This pair of dolls reveals a lot about the traditional wearing apparel of Lakota women and men. The artist included signatures of both gender roles—a baby carrier on the back of the woman and a pipe and pipe bag in the man's hands.

Tanned deer hide (*Odocoileus* sp.), unidentified filling, glass, House Sparrow feather (*Passer domesticus*), brass, synthetic hair, porcupine quill (*Erethizon dorsatum*), abalone shell (*Haliotis rufescens*), dentalium shell (*Dentalium* sp.), unidentified wood, commercial cotton, commercial wool stroud, catlinite, unidentified mammal claw, steel, rayon, nylon sinew, commercial dye; avg. H 12.6 in. (avg. 17.0 W x 32.3 H cm); 35479-1 & 2

LAKOTA GIRLS PLAY WITH THEIR TOY TIPIS, ABOUT 1890.
The wooden house in the background suggests that their families are no longer living in tipis.

(Photographer unknown. Smithsonian Institution, 43,126-G)

CHILDREN: BEGINNING THE CIRCLE

All life goes around in a circle, beginning with birth, changing through the seasons, always ending with death, from which will spring new life.

ADOLF AND STAR HUNGRY WOLF, BLACKFOOT, 1992[36]

Like children everywhere, Plains children are the treasures of the tribe. Traditionally they began life wrapped snugly in a lovingly decorated baby carrier made by a paternal aunt or a grandmother.

Women embroidered prayers for protection and long life into the things they made for their children. Each child received a decorated navel amulet containing his or her dried umbilical cord. Alice New Holy, Oglala Lakota, laments that today a child's cord is often thrown away. She asks, *How will the child know where he is?* [37]

Clothing revealed a child's place in society. A family might announce the special status of its infant by making several baby carriers as the child grew. One lucky baby received twenty-two cradles.[38]

The playthings that parents provided taught children the social roles they were expected to assume when they grew up. Mothers made miniature versions of women's equipment for their daughters to play with while practicing for their future roles.

My chum and I each had doll cradles which were beaded. . . . We also had play-tepees and poles. Whenever the camp broke for a move we were made to take care of our playthings, that is, to bundle them up and to see that they were properly packed on the travois [horse-drawn carrier], and when camp was pitched it was also our duty to unpack them and to place them in our tepees where they ought to be.

AN ARAPAHO WOMAN, 1933[39]

GIRLS' BALLS
Lakota, collected ca. 1890

These beaded balls were made for Lakota girls' puberty ceremonies. At the end of the four days of seclusion and the Buffalo Ceremony, which marked a girl's transition into womanhood, the initiate performed the Throwing-of-the-Ball.

I took the ball, and they picked the girl to receive it. And so she came up, and I had to throw that ball and she was supposed to catch it. They said it was bad luck to drop it—what kind I don't know.

NELLIE STAR BOY MENARD, LAKOTA, 1993[40]

Unidentified filling, tanned hide, commercial wool stroud, glass, commercial cotton, sinew, commercial dye; avg. D 2.5 in. (avg. 6.3 D cm); 14526-81, 82, & 83, gift of Earle Sidney Crannell

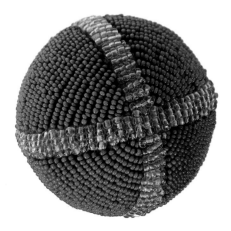

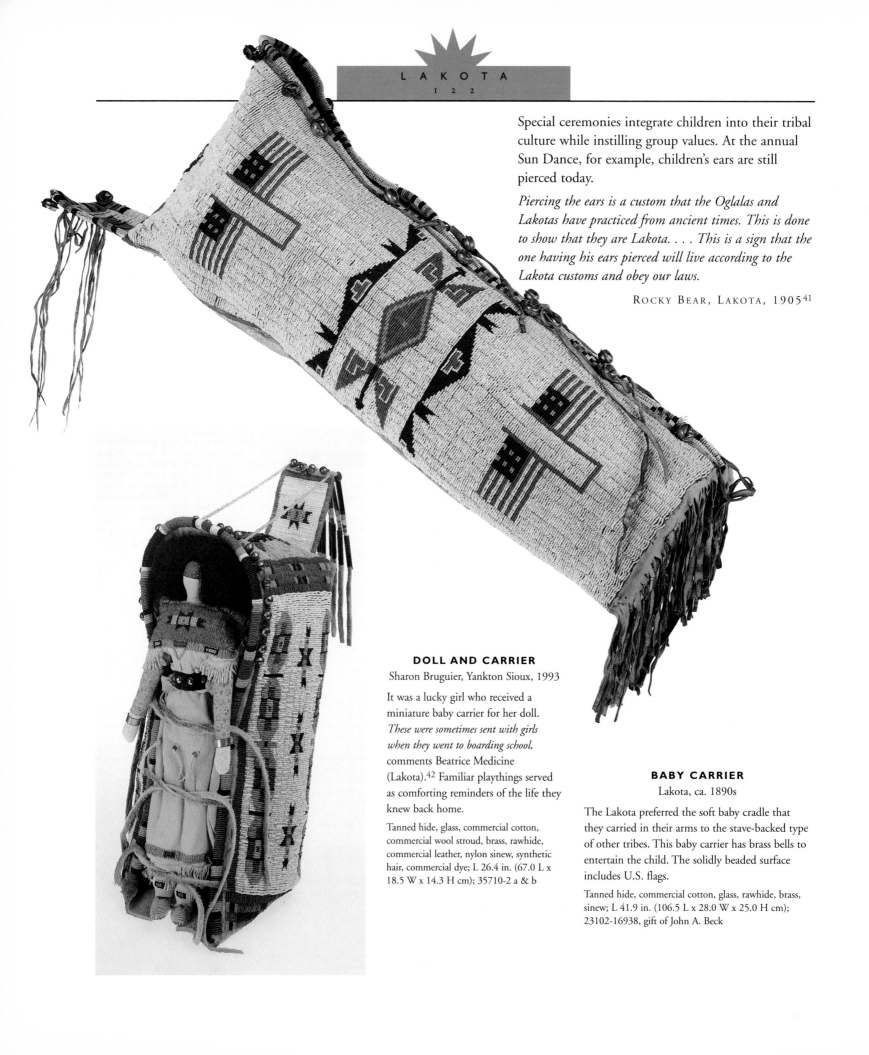

Special ceremonies integrate children into their tribal culture while instilling group values. At the annual Sun Dance, for example, children's ears are still pierced today.

Piercing the ears is a custom that the Oglalas and Lakotas have practiced from ancient times. This is done to show that they are Lakota. . . . This is a sign that the one having his ears pierced will live according to the Lakota customs and obey our laws.

ROCKY BEAR, LAKOTA, 1905[41]

DOLL AND CARRIER

Sharon Bruguier, Yankton Sioux, 1993

It was a lucky girl who received a miniature baby carrier for her doll. *These were sometimes sent with girls when they went to boarding school,* comments Beatrice Medicine (Lakota).[42] Familiar playthings served as comforting reminders of the life they knew back home.

Tanned hide, glass, commercial cotton, commercial wool stroud, brass, rawhide, commercial leather, nylon sinew, synthetic hair, commercial dye; L 26.4 in. (67.0 L x 18.5 W x 14.3 H cm); 35710-2 a & b

BABY CARRIER

Lakota, ca. 1890s

The Lakota preferred the soft baby cradle that they carried in their arms to the stave-backed type of other tribes. This baby carrier has brass bells to entertain the child. The solidly beaded surface includes U.S. flags.

Tanned hide, commercial cotton, glass, rawhide, brass, sinew; L 41.9 in. (106.5 L x 28.0 W x 25.0 H cm); 23102-16938, gift of John A. Beck

BABY BONNET
Lakota, collected ca. 1890

BOY'S MOCCASINS
Lakota, collected ca. 1890

AMULET
Alice New Holy (1925-), Oglala Lakota, Pine Ridge Reservation, South Dakota, 1992

Protection—whether it be from the elements or spiritual protection—is a theme in Lakota children's clothing. Lakota mothers thought the Euro-American-style sunbonnet, like the umbrella, was quite sensible on the treeless Plains. They preferred, however, to construct bonnets from hide decorated with beads or quills, rather than from calico or other fabrics.

One mother quilled a lizard on the soles of her young son's moccasins, probably as a prayer for strength and a long life. Both the lizard and the turtle are the chosen forms for umbilical amulets. These animals are generally considered the guardians of life because of their abilities to protect themselves. The turtle's hard shell provides complete protection when the animal withdraws into it. Some lizards shed their tails to distract predators; others change color to camouflage themselves. Thus, they are good candidates for long, safe lives.

Baby bonnet: Tanned hide, commercial cotton, glass, brass, sinew; W 5.5 in. (14.0 L x 14.0 W x 33.0 H cm); 14526-4, gift of Earle Sidney Crannell

Boy's moccasins: Tanned hide, porcupine quill (*Erethizon dorsatum*), glass, commercial cotton, sinew, commercial dye; L 4.7 in. (12.0 L x 5.0 W x 5.0 H cm); 14526-22 a & b, gift of Earle Sidney Crannell

Amulet: Tanned hide, porcupine quill (*Erethizon dorsatum*), immature mountain goat? hoof (*Oreamnos americanus*), sinew, commercial dye; L 6.1 in. (15.5 L x 8.7 W cm); 35415-8

WARRIORS: A FEATHER I SEEK [43]

The Indian is always feathered up; he is a relative to the wings of the air.

BLACK ELK, LAKOTA, 1944 [44]

Because birds soar in the sky realm where the supernaturals dwell, they have the ability to carry messages between these lofty deities and earthbound humans. Possessing such powers, birds are sought as personal guardian spirits in visions or dreams. Personal talismans, such as bird feathers, claws, or bones, give evidence that the bearer has received such a patron.

Prized above all is the eagle. When a Lakota man was selected as a chief, *he was reminded that he must be like the eagle, for the eagle is the chief of all birds, its feathers are the rewards of valor, it flies highest. A chief should study to resemble the eagle.*[45]

On one occasion Sitting Bull received a magnificent eagle feather bonnet with a double trailer of tail feathers. *Every feather in that bonnet represented some brave deed, some "coup" performed by the warrior who had contributed it. It was in fact the symbol of the combined valor of the Northern Teton Sioux.*[45]

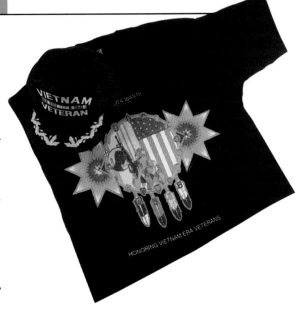

T-SHIRT
Martin Red Bear, Oglala/Brulé Lakota, Pine Ridge Reservation, South Dakota, 1991

CAP
Collected 1995

On Lakota reservations visible signs of participation in the armed services are everywhere. Residents wear T-shirts, caps, and jackets commemorating their service. Living rooms and bedrooms are filled with photos and memorabilia of the military experiences of family members, both male and female.

T-shirt: Commercial cotton, ink; W 33.0 in. (80.1 L x 83.9 W cm); 35976-1. Cap: Polyester, commercial cotton, nylon, plastic, metal alloy; L 10.2 in. (26.0 L x 18.5 W x 12.0 H cm); 36076-1, gift of Bill Menard, Sicangu (Brulé) Lakota Vietnam veteran

SHIRT
Lakota, ca. 1880s

Special shirts such as this one were originally meant to be worn by four leading men of each Lakota band. After the move to the reservation, however, these garments lost their exclusivity. They are distinguished by the hair fringe on each sleeve, originally emblematic of enemy scalps taken in battle. The hair was generally donated by women in mourning, who cut off all their hair, or even taken from a horse's tail. This shirt reputedly belonged to Red Cloud.

Tanned hide, glass, human hair, horsehair (*Equus caballus*), commercial wool stroud, sinew, ochre, paint, commercial dye; L 61.0 in. (107.0 L x 155.0 W cm); 23102-16844, gift of John A. Beck

ON THE CROW CREEK RESERVATION IN SOUTH DAKOTA, A SIGN PROMINENTLY DISPLAYS SUPPORT FOR HOMETOWN TROOPS ENGAGED IN DESERT STORM, 1991.

(Photo by Marsha C. Bol. Carnegie Museum of Natural History)

Feathers predominate in the paraphernalia of Plains men, and the eagle feather bonnet has become the most recognized symbol of the American Indian. Traditionally, only men of honor with accomplishments in warfare were eligible to wear these bonnets.

The Plains Indian Wars ended in 1890 with the massacre at Wounded Knee. After that there was no longer a role for warriors. The warriors' continuing emotional needs, however, resulted in great frustration. Young men could not fulfill the requirements necessary for warriors to attain positions of honor, leadership, and the right to wear the meaningful eagle feathers.

In the twentieth century, by serving in the U.S. military, Plains men—and many other American Indians—have found an opportunity to continue the warrior life. Servicemen receive the same respect once given to warriors on horseback.

World War II revitalized the culture. Men could resume their warrior status, says Joe Medicine Crow of the Crow nation.[47] Joe knows this from personal experience. During World War II while fighting the Germans, he unknowingly completed the four requirements to become a chief. He led a war party—a squad—across German lines. He touched an enemy and took his weapon while engaged in hand-to-hand combat with a German soldier. Joe even stole enemy horses when he took off with some German officers' mounts.

JOHN GRASS, LAKOTA, POSES WITH AN ELABORATE FEATHER BONNET, 1912. It is constructed from dozens of tail feathers from an immature Golden Eagle (*Aquila chrysaetos*), the feather preferred by the Lakota.

(Photo by DeLancey Gill. Smithsonian Institution, 3115-a)

Today veterans have honored roles in family and tribal life. Photographs of family members in uniform are prominently displayed in Lakota homes as a source of pride. During powwows, veterans are asked to be flag bearers, called upon to retrieve dropped eagle feathers, and honored in special veterans' songs and dances.

No other culture in our country honors their veterans as much as we American Indians do, Devil's Lake Sioux tribal chairman Peter Belgarde, Jr., announced to the audience at the 1992 United Tribes International Powwow.

BILL MENARD'S VETERAN CAP SITS ON DISPLAY IN NELLIE MENARD'S LIVING ROOM, ROSEBUD, SOUTH DAKOTA, 1995. Other memorabilia include a photo of a granddaughter, Juanita Bonhorst, in military uniform.

(Photo by Melinda McNaugher. Carnegie Museum of Natural History)

HEADDRESS AND TRAILER
Lakota, Pine Ridge Reservation, South Dakota, ca. 1910

After the close of the Plains Indian Wars, tribal regulations concerning the right to wear warbonnets were relaxed. No longer did a man wear a feather headdress only because of his many brave deeds in battle. Elaborate bonnets assumed new generalized roles and were frequently worn at community events as badges of honor and recognition.

Tanned hide, adult Golden Eagle feather (*Aquila chrysaetos*), Great Horned Owl feather (*Bubo virginianus*), Crow feather (*Corvus brachyrhynchos*), glass, horsehair (*Equus caballus*), sinew, sealing wax, commercial wool stroud, commercial cotton, commercial dye; L 92.5 in. (235.0 L x 85.0 W cm); 35153-16 & 18, gift of Albert Miller

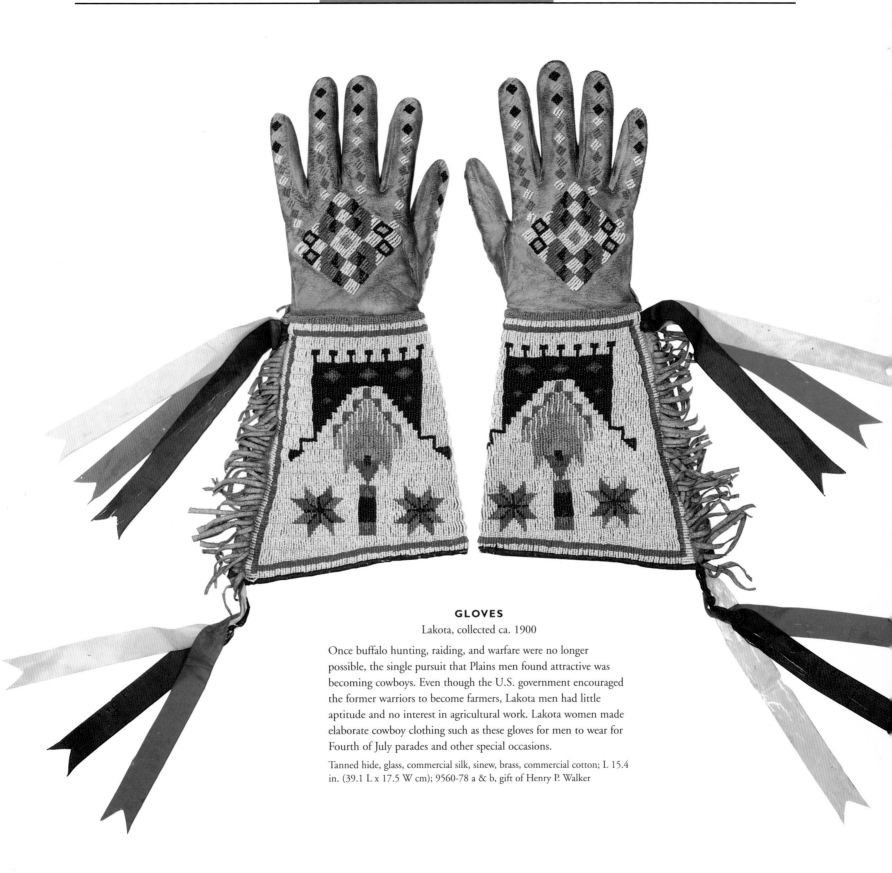

GLOVES

Lakota, collected ca. 1900

Once buffalo hunting, raiding, and warfare were no longer possible, the single pursuit that Plains men found attractive was becoming cowboys. Even though the U.S. government encouraged the former warriors to become farmers, Lakota men had little aptitude and no interest in agricultural work. Lakota women made elaborate cowboy clothing such as these gloves for men to wear for Fourth of July parades and other special occasions.

Tanned hide, glass, commercial silk, sinew, brass, commercial cotton; L 15.4 in. (39.1 L x 17.5 W cm); 9560-78 a & b, gift of Henry P. Walker

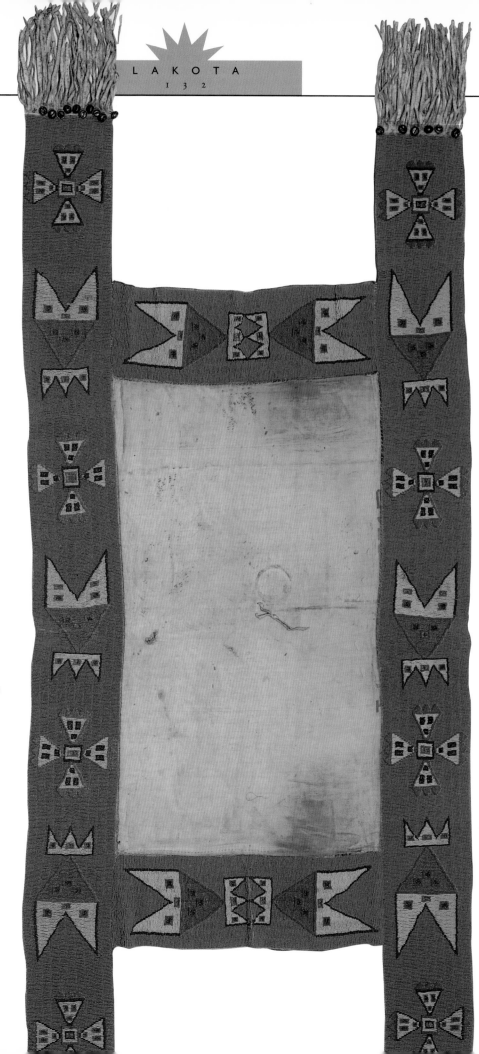

SADDLE BLANKET

Lakota, collected 1890

Although this appears to be a typical beaded saddle blanket, the central panel is a flour sack. In the last quarter of the nineteenth century, commodities were introduced through trade and annuity payments from the U.S. government. Plains women integrated newly available products into their works. Sometimes the flour sack was considered more valuable than the flour, which the Plains people had no use for in their traditional diet.

Tanned hide, glass, commercial cotton, brass, sinew, steel, ink; W 74.0 in. (73.5 L x 188.0 W cm); 14862-3, gift of Mrs. John F. Walton and Mrs. Thomas Hitchcock

"ONE TOO MANY FRY BREADS" PIN

Zia Graphics, Albuquerque, New Mexico, 1993

Paper, steel, plastic, ink; L 2.1 in. (5.4 L x 5.4 W cm); 35710-1

ARIZONA, COLORADO, AND NEW MEXICO

Too Much Fry Bread

Fry bread is one of the most popular modern Native American foods. All across America women fry great quantities for snacks, feasts, and powwows. As a cultural identifier, it has become the source for Native humor in jokes, cartoons, bumper stickers, and other expressions of popular culture.

The fry bread jokes address an issue that plagues Native Americans nationwide today. An alarmingly high rate of diabetes among Native people has resulted from a diet of white bread, foods fried in lard, commodity foods, soda pop, and sweets, along with a sedentary lifestyle. As a population, American Indians have a genetic predisposition to the disease, although its rate of occurrence varies between tribes. Among the O'odham (Pimas and Papagos) of Arizona, more than 50 percent of all adults over thirty-five have the disease. This epidemic was triggered by the change from indigenous foods to purchased foods that began in the early 1940s.

"FRY BREAD POWER" BUMPER STICKER

Western Trading Post, Inc., Denver, Colorado, ca. 1992

Paper, adhesive, ink; L 14.8 in. (38.0 L x 9.8 W cm); P-1995-27

COCHITI DOUGH BOWL

Cochiti, New Mexico, ca. 1890-1900

Clay, paint; D 12.6 in. (20.5 H x 32.2 D cm); 35652-1, gift of William B. and Gale D. Simmons

LARD CAN

Arizona, 1900s

Steel, copper, paint; D 8.4 in. (21.0 H x 21.5 D cm); 35154-8 a & b

STUDENT BODY OF CARLISLE INDIAN SCHOOL, CA. 1900.

(Photo by Maynard Hoover. Cumberland County Historical Society, 324-B)

THE CARLISLE ARROW AND RED MAN MAGAZINE, JUNE 7, 1918

Carlisle Indian Press, Carlisle Indian School, Carlisle, Pennsylvania, 1918

The school publication, printed by the students, contained articles written by them under the watchful eye of the school superintendent. The publication served as a propaganda tool for promoting the school's educational philosophies, which in turn were based on the U.S. government's ideology at the time.

The cover of this issue illustrates one of these philosophies—the students' conversion from indigenous livelihoods to the Euro-American rural farming economy. Agriculture represented an entire set of underlying white societal values—private land ownership, hard work to accumulate capital, and self-sufficient individualism—that the school sought to instill in the students. All of these precepts, however, were contrary to basic indigenous philosophies. Note the motto at the bottom of the cover.

Paper, ink, steel; L 11.0 in. (28.0 L x 20.5 W cm); 35835-15, gift of Verna Moses

STUDENT BAKING APPRENTICES AT CARLISLE INDIAN SCHOOL, CA. 1879-1902. Carlisle students spent half of each day in classes and the other half laboring at school chores and learning a trade. Boys selected such trades as baking, blacksmithing, carpentry, masonry, painting, plumbing, and printing. Girls were expected to learn the domestic arts, such as sewing, cooking, nursing, and child care. The school depended on student labor in the laundry, kitchen, and dining room. Students sewed all their uniforms and made all their shoes.

(Photo by J. H. Choate. Cumberland County Historical Society, CS-CH-99)

MATH CLASS AT CARLISLE INDIAN SCHOOL, 1901. In the early days at Carlisle, students were expected to stay for three years. Later their required term increased to five years, although students were encouraged to remain until they graduated upon completing the tenth grade. The curriculum included English, geography, history, math, and sciences.

(Photo by F. Johnston. Cumberland County Historical Society, JO-2-3)

COMING TO THE CITY

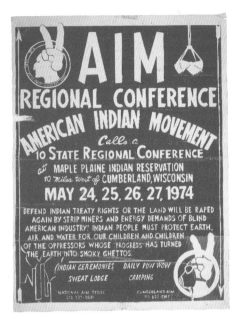

AIM POSTER

American Indian Movement, Maple Plaine Indian Reservation, Wisconsin, 1974

In the late 1960s frustrated young urban Indians began to form organizations to challenge public policy and social injustice. The American Indian Movement (AIM), founded by a group of Minneapolis Indians in 1968, became the most famous militant organization of the Red Power movement.

Paper, ink; L 22.4 in. (57.0 L x 43.0 W cm); 35834-1, gift of Michele J. Leonard

We have a lot of intact Indian cultures that are not land-based at all anymore.

ANNE ARNOLD, SPOKANE/AFRICAN AMERICAN, 1998[7]

After leaving Carlisle in 1897 I went to Steelton, where I applied for a job in the Pennsylvania Steel Company. . . . They said that so far as they knew I was the first Indian to work in a steel mill.

JASON BETZINEZ, APACHE, 1959[8]

Like some of his Carlisle classmates, Betzinez chose not to return home after his years away at boarding school. Instead, aided by his proficiency in English, he went to an urban area to find work.

Fifty years later Indian veterans returning from World War II faced a similar situation. Their experiences around the globe had changed them. Some, finding that they no longer felt at home on the reservation, headed to the cities to begin new lives.

Since the end of World War II, there has been a large-scale movement of Indian people away from the reservations to urban areas. Today more than 60 percent of the American Indian population live in cities.

A 1970 PROTEST AGAINST U.S. FEDERAL POLICIES IN DENVER, COLORADO.

(Photographer unknown. Denver Public Library, Western History Department, 14047)

The U.S. government encouraged the urban migration in the 1950s by developing a federal relocation program. The aim was to attract Indian people to the cities, where jobs were more readily available than on the reservations. Thousands of Native people responded to the promise of "good jobs" and "happy homes" as advertised in the governmental brochures.

For many, relocation was a failure. What they found, in general, were low-paying jobs and high-cost rents. Although some stayed and built a life, many returned to the reservations.

Unfamiliar challenges confront Native people who move to urban areas. Life in the city often means living next door to non-Indian strangers. It means trying to balance ones traditional cultural values with the often-conflicting requirements for success in mainstream society. *We're schizophrenics,* says Lisa Mitten, Mohawk.[9] *We are constantly walking a double road,* adds Tomi Simms, Seminole / Upper Cumberland.[10]

Issues of identity take center stage in the city. How or even whether to reveal ones identity becomes a question. *It's not uncommon to not know that your next door neighbor is Native,* remarks Russell Simms, Seminole / Upper Cumberland.[11]

What does an Indian person look like, what does a Black Indian person look like, and what does a White Indian person look like? If an Indian person doesn't have traditional Indian features, does that mean he or she is not an Indian person? These are the kinds of basic issues that we've begun to deal with here, especially in the East.

ANNE ARNOLD,
SPOKANE/AFRICAN AMERICAN,
1998[12]

Where does an Indian person go to find other Native people in a vast metropolis? To meet this need for community among otherwise scattered individuals and families, Indian centers have sprung up in the large cities, including Pittsburgh.

We've found that the Indian Center was just as important as it could be to underwrite our sense of identity. The Indian Center has provided so many ways for us to express our Indianness, says Anne Arnold, chairperson, Council of Three Rivers American Indian Center in Pittsburgh.[13]

We have so many [different types of] Indian people in this country. We have Indian people who are federally recognized members of Indian tribes; . . . we have Indian people who are not federally recognized but no less Indian; and we have Indian people who don't meet the blood quantum criteria for enrollment in their tribe, but who may, paradoxically, be so-called full-blood Indians but may be such a mixture of tribes that they cannot enroll with any particular tribe. So if you ask sixteen different people what an Indian is, you'll probably get sixteen different answers.

ANNE ARNOLD, SPOKANE/
AFRICAN-AMERICAN, 1998[14]

THE COUNCIL OF THREE RIVERS AMERICAN INDIAN CENTER, ESTABLISHED IN 1967-1968, IS THE SITE OF THE ANNUAL PITTSBURGH POWWOW, 1992.

(Photo by James B. Richardson III. Carnegie Museum of Natural History)

ELMER WHITNEY WORKING ON AN AIRCRAFT ASSEMBLY LINE IN CALIFORNIA, ABOUT 1950s

(Photographer unknown. National Archives and Records Administration, Pacific Region, 721.32)

AN INDIAN COUPLE IN DOWNTOWN MINNEAPOLIS IN 1981.

(Photo by J. Hubbard. UPI/Corbis-Bettmann Archives, U2065234.1)

JESSICA MITTEN, MOHAWK/SENECA, AGE 13, AT
THE 1992 PITTSBURGH POWWOW.

(Photo by Marsha C. Bol. Carnegie Museum of Natural History)

COUNCIL OF THREE RIVERS
POWWOW POSTER

Council of Three Rivers American Indian
Center, Inc., Pittsburgh, Pennsylvania, 1992

The reasons for the urban powwow and the reservation powwow differ. Urban powwows are more generic. Reservation ones are more tribal specific, comments Lisa Mitten, Mohawk.[15] *Reservation powwows are an annual call to home,* adds Michele Leonard, Shinnecock. *The powwow may be the only time when tribal members living in the city see family for a whole year.*[16]

Since 1978 the Indian Center in Pittsburgh has held an annual powwow. This major public event helps define the Native community as an ethnic group. Council members agree that the powwow is an opportunity to reaffirm and exhibit ethnic pride as well as a chance for urban Indians to either sustain or forge a link with their heritage.

Cardboard, ink; L 22.0 in. (56.0 L x 35.6 W cm);
P-1995-30a

★ 14TH ANNUAL ★
AMERICAN INDIAN
POW WOW

FREE
PARKING

RAIN OR
SHINE

SEPT. 26 & 27
— SAT. & SUN. 12 NOON - 7 PM —
COUNCIL OF THREE RIVERS
AMERICAN INDIAN CENTER INC.
200 Charles St. ✦ DORSEYVILLE
Take Saxonburg Blvd. To Charles St. Near Hartwood Acres
〰〰〰 FEATURING 〰〰〰
ARTS & CRAFTS ✦ NATIVE FOODS ✦ JEWELRY
COMPETITION DANCING ✦ CULTURAL DEMONSTRATIONS

OPEN TO THE PUBLIC

Donation - Adults: $4.00 ✦ Children Under 12: $2.00 ✦ Elders: $2.00
NO Drugs Or Alcohol Allowed 782 - 4457

TRIANGLE POSTER CO. PGH. PA (412) 371-0774

On the Reservation

The Civil Rights movement in the 1960s awakened activists on the reservations as well as in the cities. *During the era of the 60s, self-determination and pride came into full force,* remarks Pam Soeder, Muskogee Creek.[17]

Indian people on reservations began to express themselves openly about issues important to their lives. Baseball caps and T-shirts sometimes carry these messages. "Read our lips" aims President George Bush's words back to him and refers to the Lakotas' rights to the sacred Black Hills, which they refuse to relinquish for a cash settlement from the federal government.

Another trend on the reservations resulted from the 1980s federal funding cuts of almost 40 percent to the tribes. Forced to search for other forms of revenue, a growing number of reservations have built gaming casinos. Although these enterprises have been controversial, in some regions of the country the results have been phenomenal, providing badly needed jobs and stimulating the tribal economy.

"I LOVE BINGO" SWEATSHIRT
Kwakwaka'wakw (Kwakiutl), Alert Bay, British Columbia, Canada, 1992

Commercial cotton and polyester?, ink; W 68.0 in. (71.6 L x 172.8 W cm); 35412-7

"READ OUR LIPS" CAP
Marty White Thunder, Pine Ridge Reservation, South Dakota, Lakota, 1992

Commercial nylon?, glass, plastic, ink, copper?; L 10.6 in. (27.0 L x 22.5 W x 13.5 H cm); 35415-1

SALAMANCA MUG
Salamanca, New York, Seneca, ca. 1992

Ceramic, ink; L 4.4 in. (11.5 L x 8.6 W x 8.8 H cm); 35939-20

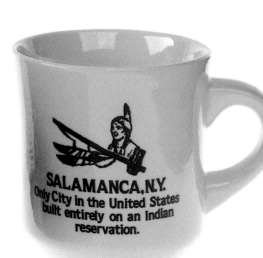

JINGLE DRESS POWWOW OUTFIT

Grace B. Gillette, Denver, Colorado,
Arikara, 1995

Grace Gillette made this outfit with its 291 jingles. She says: *The dress is styled by what I remember seeing at War Bonnet Dances and other celebrations while I was growing up [at Fort Berthold Reservation, North Dakota]. The most tedious is preparing the jingles. It takes about seven minutes to cut the lip off the [snuff can] lid, shape it, and add the bias tape for each jingle.*[18]

Ms. Gillette is the executive director of the Denver powwow, one of the largest powwows in the nation, held every March.

Commercial cotton, tinned metal; blouse: L 40.1 in. (102.0 L x 92.0 W cm); skirt: L 30.7 in. (78.0 L x 58.5 W cm); 36081-1 a & b

THE FIRST PITTSBURGH POWWOW, HELD BY THE COUNCIL OF THREE RIVERS AMERICAN INDIAN CENTER IN 1978.

(Photographer unknown. Courtesy of Tomi "Soaring Eagle" Simms)

POWWOW PROGRAMS (CLOCKWISE FROM TOP)

Bismarck, North Dakota, 1992

Albuquerque, New Mexico, 1993

Pittsburgh, Pennsylvania, 1991

Six Nations Reserve, Ontario, Canada, 1992

(Clockwise from top) Paper, ink, adhesive; L 11.0 in. (28.0 L x 21.5 W cm); P-1995-44. Paper, ink, steel?; L 10.6 in. (27.2 L x 21.0 W cm); P-1995-20. Paper, ink, steel; L 8.2 in. (21.2 L x 17.5 W cm); P-1995-45.0. Paper, ink, steel?; L 8.3 in. (21.5 L x 14.0 W cm); P-1995-19

THANKSGIVING SCENE T-SHIRT

Harold (Jack) Johnson, Six Nations Reserve, Ontario, Canada, Mohawk, 1992

Commercial cotton and polyester, ink; W 31.5 in. (75.0 L x 80.0 W cm); 35732-3

"HONOR INDIAN TREATIES" BUMPER STICKER

Location unknown, 1992

"SINCE THEIR ARRIVAL" BUMPER STICKER

Redtail, 1992

"INDIANS DISCOVERED COLUMBUS" BUMPER STICKER

Western Trading Post, Inc., Denver, Colorado, 1992

The 1992 Columbian Quincentenary sparked responses from Native people about Columbus's arrival that countered the viewpoint of mainstream society.

(From top) Paper, ink, adhesive; W 14.9 in. (9.8 L x 38.0 W cm); P-1995-26. Paper, ink, adhesive; W 10.6 in. (9.9 L x 27.1 W cm); P-1995-35. Paper, ink, adhesive; W 11.4 in. (7.5 L x 29.1 W cm); 35733-3

BEADED JFK PICTURE

Henrietta, Oklahoma, 1960s?

President John F. Kennedy is a popular figure among Indian people. During his administration in the early 1960s, he was an advocate on their behalf. He increased government funding for social services, encouraged greater tribal self-determination, and sounded the death knell for the federal policy of termination of the tribes.

Glass, commercial cotton, cardboard, commercial wool?, plastic; L 13.3 in. (34.0 L x 29.5 W x 1.0 H cm); 35567-1

Index

ERRATA

The scientific names for the following plants and animal are correct as follows:
Pages xi, 34, 41, 45, 48: rabbit brush *(Chrysothamnus nauseosus)*
Pages 16, 23, 24: maple *(Acer* sp.)
Page 24: Boreal Toad *(Bufo boreas boreas)*
Page 39: sedge root *(Carex* sp.); willow *(Salix* sp.)
Pages 58, 77: hazel *(Corylus cornuta* subsp. *californica)*
Page 76: elm bark *(Ulmus americana)*
Page 77: hemp *(Apocynum cannabinum)*

Page 111: The common name of *Terrapene ornata* is Ornate Box Turtle.